HOMETECH INDUSTRY IN GLOBAL MARKET

HOMETECH INDUSTRY
IN
GLOBAL MARKET

By

Dr. Asiya Chaudhary
Associate Professor
Dept. of Commerce
A.M.U. Aligarh (U.P.)
(INDIA)

DISCOVERY PUBLISHING HOUSE PVT. LTD.
NEW DELHI-110 002

Published by:

Namit Wasan

DISCOVERY PUBLISHING HOUSE PVT. LTD.

4383/4B, Ansari Road, Darya Ganj

New Delhi-110 002 (India)

Phone : +91-11-23279245, 43596064-65

Fax : +91-11-23253475

E-mail : discoverypublishinghouse@gmail.com
namitwasan9@gmail.com
sales@discoverypublishinggroup.com

web : www.discoverypublishinggroup.com

First Edition: **2016**

ISBN: 978-93-5056-773-9

Hometech Industry in Global Market

Printed at:

Infinity Imaging Systems

Delhi

Preface

The Indian Textiles Industry has an overwhelming presence in the economic life of the country. It is not only providing one of the basic necessities of life but also plays a key role through its contribution to industrial output, employment generation and the export earnings of the country. The Textile industry is not only experiencing for clothing application but also continuing a major outlook towards non-clothing application of textiles known as Technical textiles. These textiles are accounted to be the fastest growing sector of the textile industry which is manufacturing high tech, high performance fabric designed not just to look attractive, but to present a significant added value in terms of functionality. Technical textiles are now providing more than half of total textile production because it is growing at twice rate of textiles for clothing applications.

Depending on the product characteristics, functional requirement and end use application, the highly diversified range technical textiles products have been segmented into 12 sectors. One of the segments is Hometech (components of furniture, household textiles and floor coverings). The Home textile market is recognized as an important part of the technical textile that comprises household textiles, furnishings and upholstered furniture industry, blinds, filter cloth, mosquito nets (including fiberfill and wadding applications in bedding, cushions, sleeping bags and furniture backings). Home textiles transform a house into home by improving designs, patterns, size and styles.

Home-Tech industry has been vibrant and happening place in the textile industry in the last one decade in both India and elsewhere.The promotion of Home-tech segment of technical textile requires the setting up of centre of excellence for the home-tech products. Considering it highly skilled and technical man power and abundant availability of raw material, India can emerge as a key player on the global fronts. On the contrary it lacks behind in many aspects. Taking this as a background, it becomes necessary to assess the competitiveness of the industry so as to reveal the various prospects which are yet to be tapped in this sector.

The home tech industry is growing gradually in India. The production has improved with time but still a big quantity is imported from other countries to meet the growing demand. With the improving income levels the demand for the home tech products is surely going to rise further. This necessitates the development of stronger industry in the country, not only to fulfill its local demand but also improve the exports of the sector. The purpose of this book is to identify the salient features which matters most for improving the efficiency and competitiveness of India's Home Tech sector, identifying policy options to improve industrial production and national export performance.

The existing areas of problem are:

1. In what way the parameters export, import and production can be used to measure the trade performance of the Indian Hometech Industry in international market vis-a- vis US and China?
2. How to apply the five forces of competitive analysis existing in the Indian Hometech Industry to measure the degree of their presence and impact on the industry with the help of Porters' Model?
3. What are the areas of competitive strengths and weaknesses of the Hometech in India?
4. Why in spite of abundance of raw material trained manpower and rich inheritance in textiles, the sector is not producing enough to meet the nation's demand and why a huge quantity of Hometech products are being imported?

The book is written after substantial review of literature. The reviews expose a great contribution in respect of the earlier studies based on market size, consumption, prospects and challenges of Technical Textiles in India and abroad. Majority of the study deals with its scope, significance, necessity, advantages, government initiatives and issues concerns for low growth of the industry, but lack concerns for its growth and development in India. No work measures the exports and imports of the industry in order to analyze its status in international trade. Some of them have devoted to show the importance and demand of various segments of the technical textile industry such as Geotech, Meditech, Buildtech, Agrotech but they did not even touch the Hometech segment.

The review of literature thus reveals a gap in so far as no study is specific in dealing with the Hometech segment of the Technical textiles in India. Nor does any work reviewed tried to examine the competitiveness of the Hometech industry in India in international market in Indian Scenario. The present study is an earnest attempt in the direction of bridging this gap.

The book is divided in to five chapters. Each chapter goes deeper in to explain different aspects of Hometech Industry. The first chapter gives an overview of the Indian Technical Textiles Industry. It explains the technical textile and its different segments. The chapter also goes deeper in to explain the global scenario and the Indian scenario of the technical textiles. Further it details the factors that are responsible for the slow growth of the industry in India.

The second chapter gives an overview of the Hometech Industry, one of the strong segments of the technical textiles. It defines the various products of this segment, i.e. Fiberfil, Carpet backing cloth (Jute & Synthetic), Stuff toys, Blinds, HV AC filters, Filter cloth for vacuum cleaners, Mattress and pillow components, Nonwoven wipes, Mosquito nets and Furniture fabrics. The chapter gives the market dynamics and key growth drivers of each products. It also mentions the key manufacturers of each products in India.

The third chapter gives further details regarding the growth of the industry in the last fourteen years. The chapter brings out clearly Indian Hometech industry in international market. After analyzing the consumption and international trade of Indian Hometech industry with the world in general and USA and China in particular, it concludes that the industry in India is growing substantially to meet the demand. This can be witnessed by the improvement in production. In spite of the growth and improvement in the Indian Hometech industry we find that it still lags behind in the international market. The industry needs to grow stronger to come at par with its competitors. In order to study the industry further i.e. its strengths and weaknesses, researcher conducted the competitive analysis of the industry by applying Porter's five forces model.

Any business happens in highly complex and competitive environment. It's important to understand strengths and weaknesses of its current and potential competitors. This makes it very important for startups to understand and analyze their competitors and frame their growth strategies [both offensive and defensive] accordingly.The most influential and analytical model for assessing the nature of competition in the industry is Micheal Porter's Five Forces model, which is used in this study. The fifth chapter examines the competitiveness of the Hometech industry in India by framing various hypothesis. Out of the ten hypotheses framed, the first and the ninth are accepted and others are rejected.

After applying the Porter's Five Forces Model on Indian Hometech Industry and statistically analysing the data collected through questionnaire and drawing inferences, the last chapter gives an interpretation to the complete analysis. The interpretation done and conclusions drawn are based on quantitative as well as qualitative data. Quantitative data is statically analysed and the interpretation is based on that. At the time of filling of questionnaire few respondents were hesitant to disclose the facts. The discussions with them added qualitatively to the researcher's data bank. The chapter further extends to give suggestions and recommendations for strengthening of the industry.

–Author

Contents

	Preface	
	Abbreviations	
1.	Indian Technical Textiles Industry	1-23
2.	Hometech Industry in India	24-44
3.	Growth of the Hometech Industry in India	45-55
4.	Competitive Analysis of Indian Hometech Industry	56-70
5.	Interpretation, Problems and Recommendations	71-100
	Bibliography	101-118
	Index	119-122

Abbreviations

G.D.P: Gross Domestic Products
IR and **UV Rays:** Infrared and Ultraviolet Rays
NBC Suits: Nuclear, Biological, Chemical Suits
NVH: Noise Vibration and Harness
HDPE: High-density Polyethylene
AGM: Absorptive Glass Mat
SFIT: Smart Fabrics and Interactive Textiles
IT: Information Technology
US: United States of America
EU: European Union
UAE: United Arab Emirates
CBC: Carpet Backing Cloth
CAGR: Compound Annual Growth Rate
USD: United States Dollar
TT: Technical Textiles
TE: Textiles Exchange
FIBC: Flexible Intermediate Bulk Containers
NBC: National Building Code
GST: Goods & Service Tax
HV AC: Heating, Ventilating and Air-conditioning
Virgin PSF Fiberfil: Virgin Polyester Staple Fiber Fill
HEPA Filters: High Efficiency Particulate Air Filters

PU Coated: Polyurethanecoated

DGCIS: Directorate General of Commercial Intelligence and Statistics

H_0: Hypothesis

ANOVA: Analysis of variance (ANOVA) is a collection of statistical models used in order to analyze the differences among group means and their associated procedures (such as "variation" among and between groups), developed by statistician and evolutionary biologist Ronald Fisher.Sig.: Significance level

Std.: Standard

MFA: Multi Fiber Agreement

COE: Centers of Excellences

BTRA: The Bombay Textile Research Association

SASMIRA: The Synthetic & Art Silk Mills' Research Association

SITRA: South Indian Textiles Research Association

NITRA: North India Textiles Research Association

ATIRA: Ahamdabad Textiles Industries Research Association

SEZ: Special Economic Zone

FTZ: Free Trade Zone

R & D: Research & Development

CHAPTER 1

Indian Technical Textiles Industry

INTRODUCTION

Generally, textile industry is considered as an industry fulfilling clothing requirements of human beings for protection, grace, and to improve aesthetic sense. This sector is known as traditional textile or general textile. On the other hand, textile is also used for specific purposes; use of textile in industry, for human protection from extreme situation. This sector has many names but the most common are technical textile, industrial textile, and functional textile. Keeping in view the usages of textile, we can divide textile into two main sectors; traditional textile and technical textile. Traditional textile deals with the general demands of human being, mainly it covers clothing, made ups, bed wears, etc. whereas, technical textile is a product made to serve a particular and technical requirement; water proof jackets, filters, fire proof seats etc.

TEXTILES INDUSTRY

The textiles Industry fulfills the physiological needs of mankind and therefore touches the lives in one or the other way. The textile Industry is primarily concerned with the production of yarn and cloth and the subsequent design of clothing and their distribution including local and global market. The raw material may be natural or synthetic using products of the chemical industry. Indian Textile Industry is one of the leading textile industries in the world. Though was predominantly unorganized industry even a few years back, but the scenario started changing after the economic liberalization in 1991. The opening up of economy gave the much- needed thrust to the Indian textile industry, which has now successfully become one of the largest in the world.

Indian textile industry plays a major role in the economy of the country. The industry contributes about 14% to industry production, 4% to country's G.D.P & 17% to country's export earnings. Indian textile industry is also the largest in the country in terms of employment generation. It not only generates jobs in its own industry, but also opens up scopes for the other ancillary sectors. The sector employs nearly 35 million people and after agriculture, is the second highest employer in the country. India has the largest area under cotton cultivation- a million hectares- constituting 25% of the world's total cultivation area. It is largest producer of raw cotton and jute (1900 Mn kg). It is 2nd largest producer of cotton yarn (2700 Mn kg), cellulose fibre/ yarn and also 2nd largest producer of silk (15 Mn kg). (Advantage India' – Textiles for apparel, VOL II, India Brand Equity foundation (IBEF) www.ibef.org)

TECHNICAL TEXTILES: MEANING AND CONCEPT

Technical and textiles are two words that when combined resonate with opportunity for a growing number of companies in the textile industry. Other terms such as industrial, specialty, performance and engineered textiles may also be used in some markets, but technical textiles encompass each of these areas. Technical textiles are predominately characterized as having specific performance-based attributes and typically must meet established performance specification criteria. Tensile strength and elongation, weight, elasticity, resistance to flammability and high heat levels, moisture-transport capabilities, durability, and weather ability are some examples of attributes that could be included in a technical textiles performance specification. As can be expected, the technical textiles industry is as broad and diverse as the products it generates, with new and innovative applications being developed on a daily basis.

(Opportunities Abound For Technical Textiles- By Jim Kaufman and Sean Kroszner, http://www.textileworld.com/Issues/2007/May-June/Nonwovens- Technical_Textiles/Opportunities _Abound_For_Technical_Textiles)

"Comprising all those textiles based products which are used principally for their performance or functional characteristics rather than for their aesthetics or are used for non – consumer (i.e. industrial) application"

By David Rigby Associates (David Rigby Associates is a consultancy specializing in the fiber, textiles and clothing industry, based in Manchester UK.)

"Technical textiles are materials meeting high technical and quality requirements, (mechanical, thermal, electrical, durability...) giving them the ability to offer technical functions"

By Nemoz (Encyclopedia Universal, (2001).)

From the above definition we may conclude that Technical textiles understood as textile materials and products used for technical performance and functional properties and are not only concerned to traditional, aesthetic or decorative characteristics. Some terms which are often used in place of technical textile are industrial textiles, functional textiles, performance textiles, engineering textiles, invisible textiles and hi-tech textiles.

Wide variety and diversity in raw material, process, product, application as well as range, these are two very important features that make it an ideal industry.

Technical textiles may be used as individually or as part or sub component of another bigger product. For example – fire retardant fabric used by fireman is an example of technical textiles used individually where as the tyre cord fabric in tyres and interlining in shirt collar are examples of technical textiles used as sub component. They are desired because of their strength, performance and other functional properties. Some areas where they are more demanded are food industry and paper mills.

Technical textiles have great features like functional requirement, health, safety, cost effectiveness, durability, high strength, light weight, versatility which makes it even more popular now a days and this is the reason for their higher growth and demand in the market.

TYPES OF TECHNICAL TEXTILES

Dr. Guy Nemoz classifies the Technical textiles into four classes based on their functions (Presentation on "Technical Textiles with focus on the use of 'Geo Textiles' 2006" by the Ministry of Textiles, 12th December):

1. Mechanical function - involves mechanical resistance reinforcement of material and elasticity.
2. Exchange function- involves filtration, insulation, drainage, impermeability and absorption.
3. Function of living being- involves antibacterial, anti dust mites, biocompatibility and bio degradability.
4. Protective function - involves electrical insulation, IR and UV rays, NBC, high visibility and electromagnetic fields.

SEGMENTS IN TECHNICAL TEXTILES

Depending on the product characteristics, functional requirement and end use application, the highly diversified range technical textiles products have been segmented into twelve sectors:

1. Agrotech (Agriculture, horticulture and forestry)
2. Buildtech (building and construction)
3. Clothtech (technical components of shoes and clothing)
4. Geotech (Geotextiles, civil engineering)
5. Hometech (components of furniture, household textiles and floor coverings)
6. Indutech (filtration, cleaning and other industrial usage)
7. Meditech (hygiene and medical)
8. Mobiltech (automobiles, shipping, railways and aerospace)
9. Oekotech (environmental protection)
10. Packtech (packaging)

11. Protech (personal and property protection)
12. Sportech (sport and leisure)

Let us know each segment:

Agrotech

Agrotech includes technical textile products used in agriculture, horticulture, floriculture, fisheries and forestry. Products covered under Agrotech are: Shade-nets, Mulch-mats, Crop-covers, Anti-hail nets and bird protection nets, Fishing nets, etc.

Meditech

Textile material used in hygiene, health and personal care are covered under this segment. Meditech products are available in knitted and non-woven forms based on area of application. e.g. Surgicalsutures, Surgical dressings, Diapers, Sanitary Napkins, etc.

Mobiltech

Products used in automotive and automotive components (including aircrafts and railways) are basically covered under this head. Mobiltech products can be divided into two groups – visible components and concealed components. The visible components include seat upholstery, carpets, seat belts, headliners, etc. The concealed components include Noise Vibration and Harness (NVH) components, tyre cords, liners, etc.

Packtech

Packaging material used in industrial, agricultural consumer and other goods comes under this head. It ranges from synthetic bags used for industrial packaging to jute sacks used for packing food grains.

Sportech

Technical textile products used in sports and leisure comes under this segment. e.g. Artificial Turf, parachute fabrics, sail cloth, ballooning fabrics etc.

Buildtech

Buildtech segment constitute of textiles or composite materials used in the construction of permanent and temporary buildings as well as structures. eg. Architectural membrane, hoarding & sign ages, cotton canvas tarpaulins, HDPE tarpaulins, etc.

Clothtech

The Clothtech segment of technical textiles majorly comprises of textile components used for specific functional applications in garments and shoes. These components are largely hidden e.g. interlinings in shirts, sewing threads, shoe laces, labels, hook and loop fasteners (Velcro), etc. Fabrics like umbrella cloth are also classified under the Clothtech segment.

Hometech

The Hometech segment of technical textiles constitute of the textile components used in household applications. The products range covers a wide area starting from blinds used in houses to the filter products used in vacuum cleaners. They are an important component in the mattress and pillows as well. They are made of both natural and synthetic fibers.

Protech

Protech is a confluence of textile products and related material used in the manufacture of various protective clothing for personnel working in hazardous environment. The protective clothing includes garments and related paraphernalia for protection from harmful chemical environment, extreme temperature environments, low visibility, ballistic protection, etc. e.g. Bullet-proof jackets Retardent apparels, NBC suits, High visibility clothing, chemical protection clothing, etc.

Geotech

As the term suggests Geotech segment comprises of technical textile products used in Geotechnical applications pertaining to soil, rock, earth etc. referred to as Geotextiles. Therefore often Geotextiles specifically refers to permeable fabric or synthetic material, woven or non-woven, which can be used with geotechnical engineering material. The principal functions performed by Geotextiles are confinement/ separation, reinforcement, filtration and drainage, and protection. e.g.

Civil engineering (roads and pavements, slope stabilization and embankment protection, tunnels, rail-track bed stabilization, ground stabilization and drainage etc), Marine Engineering (Soil Erosion control and embankment protection), Environmental Engineering(Landfills and waste management).

Oekotech

Oekotech segment refers to use of technical textiles in Environmental Engineering. The primary segment in this is Landfill waste management which refers to the use of Geosynthetic products to secure landfills against leakage of municipal or hazardous waste. Other areas include secondary protection in Chemical/Oil Industries (ground covers and the like around process tanks for secondary containment should the tanks leak). A modern engineering landfill has the following components - a basal lining system to prevent the contamination of soil, and ground water by pollutants, a capping system to seal the waste when the capacity of the landfill is exhausted, an impervious sealing layer which prevents the entry of pollutants in the ground, a leachate collection system for the collection and transmission of leachates to a collection pit, a secondary leachate collection/ leak detection system.

Indutech

Indutech includes technical textile products used in the manufacturing sector. e.g. Conveyor belt, Drive belt, Cigarette filter rods, Decasting cloth, AGM glass battery separators, Bolting cloth, etc.

SMART FABRICS AND INTERACTIVE TEXTILES (SFIT)

Apart from the technical textiles, the Global Market for Smart Fabrics and Interactive Textiles (SFIT) has developed significantly in recent years. These textiles provide interactive properties such as electrical conductivity, ballistic resistance and biological protection. Electrically heated seat kits which have been a major commercial success are a fine example of this type of textile.

INNOVATIONS IN FIBERS, TEXTILES AND APPARELS

Innovations enable a company to differentiate its products and take competitive advantage in the market. Many innovations have been made in the field of textile manufacturing such as:

1. **Fire Resistant textile** protects human skin from flames and heat, hot gases and vapors. These are used in industries like aerospace, construction, defence, fire fighting, engineering, mining etc.
2. **Smart or Intelligent textiles** can think for themselves. They can sense and react to external conditions and also retain the aesthetic and technical properties of textile material. They are used to measure strain, temperature, pressure, electric currents, magnetic fields, etc. in defence, aerospace, science and research, nuclear plants etc.
3. **Ultra-fine textiles** use tightly woven fabrics which have high resistance to dust, water and wind. They also have extremely soft look and are used in manufacture of fashion garments like suede suits etc. They are also used in medicinal field for making bandages, sheets, patients' gowns, curtains and bed sheets.
4. **Electronic textiles** or e-textiles are used for manufacturing fabrics that have electronic interconnections within them. These clothing measure blood pressure, heart rate, body temperature etc. and relay the data to a computer, cell phone or other device that could signal for help if the wearer experiences a health problem. Another variation of it may have an MP3 player fitted in it.
5. **Nano fibers** are used for manufacturing protective suits for police, defence, fire fighters etc. These fibers are the finest fibers in the world and have better mechanical properties than any micro fibers made of the same material.
6. **Abrasion resistant fabrics** can resist injury, erosion, scratch, extreme weather etc. They are used in defence, fire fighting, marine, automotive, glass manufacturing, engineering etc.

7. **Adhesives fabrics ensure** a long-lasting bonding between various elements and are used in industries like aerospace, automobile, automotive, water fabrication, IT, electrical, metal works, construction, aviation etc.
8. **Anti allergic and Anti Bacterial textiles** can reduce all types of bacterial, fungal allergies like colds and flues and improve sleep, meditation and relaxation, increases lung capacity, absorption of Vitamins B and C, relieves from migraine, respiratory tracks and nose disorders, stress, etc.
9. **Anti Magnetic textiles and Anti Radiation fabrics** offer protection against magnetic pull in areas with active magnetic field and from Ultra Violet radiations. These textiles are used in industries such as aerospace, aviation, petrochemical, textile, electronics, machinery and environment protection.
10. **Anti-static textile prevents** damage to electrical components, fires and explosions when working with flammable liquids and gases.
11. **Multifunctional Textiles** include many properties in one product. These may include functionalities including waterproof, soil repellent, fire resistance, wrinkle free, anti-U and antistatic finishing and other qualities as well.
12. **Auxetic textiles** get fatter when stretched and narrower when compressed. These are used for making Personal Protection Clothing, filtration, Mechanical Lungs, Ropes, Cords & Nets, Medical Bandages, Fibrous Seals etc.
13. **Insulating textiles** can keep away cold and damp moisture in extreme climatic conditions. These are used in manufacture of garments for areas which have temperature below 0 degree Celsius- Mountaineering apparel, Defence uniforms, Astronaut costumes etc.
14. **Luminescent and reflective textiles** can absorb and store light energy when exposed to natural and artificial light sources such as sunlight, U.V. or fluorescent light and continuously emit stored energy in a form of visible light. These textiles are used as safety wear for fire men, traffic

men and other personnel and for making warning boards or strips in industries like construction, electrical, mechanical etc.

15. **Shape memory polymer** is a significant innovation in the textile and garment industry. These intelligent textiles can remember their original shape and return to it after heat treatment like washing or treatment with steam. They can be used for textile finishing, fiber and film-making and in industries like defence and aerospace.
16. **Soluble textiles** can dissolve in water at temperature ranging from 37 to 40 degree C depending on their composition. They are sterile hygienic materials used to protect patients and medical staff from infections, surgical garments and drapes, face masks and shoe covers, food industry including food science, agriculture, ceramics, paper and ink technology and explosives.

Apart from the above innovations many other new textiles have been introduced in the market.

17. **Bio-textiles**, fitted with certain enzymes, genetically engineered microorganisms or vitamins etc. have medicinal, therapeutic and protective characteristics. These are useful in medical and defense industries.
18. **Cleansing textiles** are used for domestic, industrial, nuclear plants purposes and also in cosmetic for making skin cleansing tissues and wipes and in automobiles as dust mapping dusters.
19. **Deodorizing or Odor absorbing textiles** absorb liquids and even gases. These are used for making sportswear, under garments, socks, curtains, sheets etc. for hospitals and hotels.
20. **Anti Ballistic Textiles** are used in Defense, Police, Fire Fighting, Aerospace & Aviation etc. as protection textiles against heavy impact, bullets, stabbing etc.
21. **Waterproof textiles** are resistant to water and are used in marine and related industries, water sports, sails, protective garments, umbrellas, packaging material, field covers for cricket matches etc.

22. **Windproof textiles** are used in making wind-sheeters and jackets for bikers, in defense and aerospace industries for making special uniforms and in manufacture of sports wear for adventure sports.

TECHNICAL TEXTILES - GLOBAL SCENARIO

Technical textiles are growing in the global market at a faster rate than expected. In the global markets the US and EU remain major manufacturers and consumers of technical textiles. The Asian countries like China and India are emerging as chief producing centers. On consumption aspects, Russia is developing in to an important growing market. Turkey's technical textiles market has also started to develop in the recent years. Some of the facts related to world technical textile markets will throw some more light on the issue:

(a) According to the report the demand for technical textiles that was worth USD 133.93 billion in 2012 is expected to increase toUSD 160.38 billion by the end of 2018. In terms of volumes, the global demand is expected to reach 30.71 million tons by 2018, growing at a moderate CAGR of 3.3% from 2012 to 2018. (Global Technical Textiles Market is Expected To Reach USD 160.38 Billion By 2018: Transparency Market Research, NEW YORK, June 24, 2013/PRNewswire/—)

(b) Asia is fast emerging as the chief producer and consumer of technical textiles.

(c) The Texas Tech University has predicted the growth of nonwovens and technical textiles markets in India by 13.3% per annum during 2005-50.

(d) The demand for filters in China is forecast to rise by 14.4% a year up to 2011 due to developments in motor vehicle production, manufacturing output, construction activities, and urbanization of the population.

(e) Turkey is developing as an important center for technical textiles production and is exporting technical textile raw material and end products to the world. (Online journal:- TE Textiles Exchange: A Pageant of rich and fascinating Textiles, article: 'Technical Textiles Industry: An Overview)

The pie chart given below presents a value wise share (in terms of percent) of each segment of the technical textiles market in the year 2010. As evident from the graph below, Mobiltech, Indutech and Sportech are the largest segments of global market, together accounting for 55% of the world market.

Chart 1.1: **Value-wise share of each segment in global technical textile market (2010)**

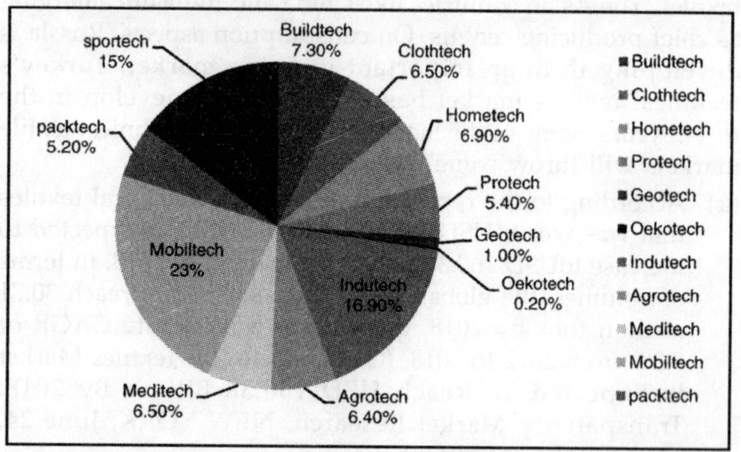

Sources: Report of the Expert Committee on Technical Textiles (ECTT) Volume – I, 'World Market Forecasts for 2010 of technical textiles and industrial nonwovens' by David Rigby Associates

From the pie chart we may infer that Mobiltech enjoys the major share of 23% in the Global market, followed by Indutech 16.90%, Sportech 15%, Buildtech 7.30%, Hometech 6.9%, Meditech and Clothtech 6.5% each, Agrotech 6.4%, Protech 5.4%, Packtech 5.2%, Geotech 1% and lastly Oekotech .20%.

The following table gives the value-wise share of each segment of the industry in the global market and its growth rate between the years.

Table 1.1: Segment-wise Global Market Size of Technical Textiles

Technical Textile Sectors	Years						
	2000		2005		2010		CAGR(%)
	Value	% to Total	Value	% to Total	Value	% to Total	Value
Mobiltech	25629	27.59	26861	25.13	29282	23.00	1.34
Indutech	13405	14.43	16687	15.61	21528	16.91	4.85
Sportech	13897	14.96	16052	15.02	19062	14.98	3.21
Buildtech	5872	6.32	7296	6.83	9325	7.33	4.73
Hometech	6750	7.27	7622	7.13	8778	6.90	2.66
Clothtech	6070	6.54	7014	6.56	836	6.53	3.19
Meditech	5391	5.80	6670	6.24	8238	6.47	4.33
Agrotech	5541	5.97	6568	6.14	8079	6.35	3.84
Protech	5193	5.59	5873	5.49	6857	5.39	2.82
Packtech	4393	4.73	5329	4.99	6630	5.21	4.20
Geotech	740	0.80	927	0.87	1203	0.95	4.98
Total	**92881**	**100.00**	**106899**	**100.00**	**127288**	**100.00**	**3.20**

Source: Ministry of Textiles. (2004, July). Report of the Expert committee on Technical Textiles: Volume-I. New Delhi: Ministry of Textiles, Government of India. Udyog Bhavan– 110 011. p. 6

The Industry has witnessed a Compound Annual Growth Rate (CAGR) of over 3% from 2000 to 2010, with Buildtech, Geotech, Oekotech and Indutech being the fastest growing segments. Going forward, the major growth areas for technical textiles in the global context are projected to be medical and personal hygiene, sports and leisure, environmental protection, pollution control and filtration, garment and shoe industry. Following table gives a view of the major Technical Textile (TT) Producing Countries.

Table 1.2: Major Technical Textile (TT) Producing Countries

Country	Technical Textile Activity
Germany	Leading TT producer and consumer in EuropeSignificant synergy with manufacturer of Textile machinery
France	380 companies active in Technical Textiles Well-financed and Well-organized Industry
Japan	Innovation and powerR&D centres and strategic production sites
UK	Around 200 medium sized Tech Tex manufacturing companies
Korea	Presence of research centers, developing brands of clothing known worldwide. Increasing the share of textiles produced for technical markets (from 25% in 2005, to 55% in 2015)
USA	Comprehensive protectionist measures since 2001Leader: automotive and industrial sectors
China	Increasingly considerably R&D targeting technical textiles
India	New government measures to support targeted growth sectors (TT and Technology Upgradation Fund Scheme)

Source: Gherzi. (2011). Technical Textiles- Raw materials & Technologies. Presented in 5th Asian Textile Conference, Mumbai – March 17-18.

The US is the largest consumer of technical textiles, followed by Western Europe and Japan. However, Technical Textile industry in the developed world is maturing in a significant way resulting in moderate growth in these economies. In contrast, China, India and other countries in Asia, America and Eastern Europe are expected to experience healthy growth in the near future. Asia is emerging as a powerhouse of both production as well as consumption of technical textiles. China, Japan, Korea, Taiwan and India have great potential to make an impact in this industry in the coming decade.

TECHNICAL TEXTILES – INDIAN SCENARIO

India is emerging as a significant player in technical textiles. The fast-paced economic growth leading to infrastructure creation as well as higher disposable income has made India a key market for the technical textile products. Moreover, the country has developed a foothold in the production of technical textiles owing to its skilled and technical manpower as well as abundant availability of raw material. More investments are underway in this sector; as per the Ministry of Textiles, as on September 2010, 26,163 applications for technical textile projects with a project cost of US$ 14.5 billion2 were disbursed under Technology Upgradation Fund Scheme (TUFS). Indian Technical Textile industry is estimated at US$ 11 billion2 (2009-10), with domestic consumption of US$ 10.3 billion. The Industry has witnessed a significant growth of 16% from 2001-02 to 2009-10 and, is expected to grow at a rate of 11% year-on year and reach a market size of US$ 15.1 billion by the year 2012-13. Domestic consumption is expected to increase to US$ 14.1 billion by the year 2012-13.

The following chart brings out the share each segment holds in India in 2009-2010:

Chart 1.2: **Value-wise share of each segment in Indian technical textile market (2009-10)**

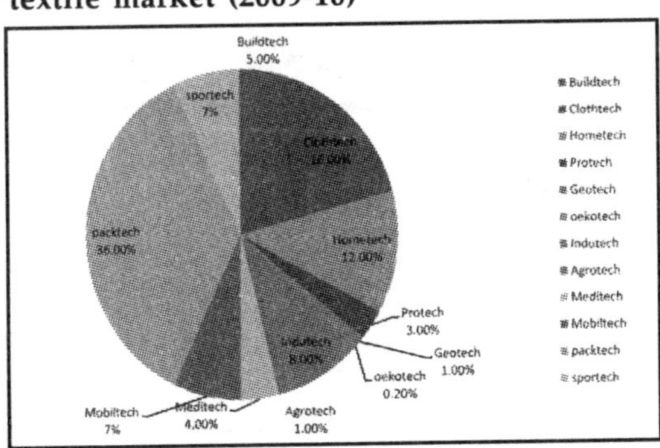

Source: Baseline survey of the Technical Textile industry in India, IMaCS Analysis

The following table gives breakup of the Technical Textiles market in India and its growth since 2007-08. It also calculates the CAGR growth rate.

Table 1.3: Break-up of Technical Textiles Market in India

Sub Segments	2007-08	2008-09	2009-10	2010-11	CAGR
Packtech	146.3	165.07	186.25	210.15	13%
Clothtech	69.08	74.72	80.81	87.41	8%
Hometech	50.25	56.14	62.73	70.08	12%
Indutech	32.06	35.63	39.60	44.02	11%
Mobiltech	31.83	35.07	38.63	42.56	10%
Sportech	28.51	31.59	35.00	38.78	11%
Buildtech	21.57	23.39	25.36	27.49	8%
Meditech	16.69	18.08	19.59	21.22	8%
Protech	13.02	14.29	15.69	17.22	10%
Agrotech	5.53	5.97	6.45	6.96	8%
Geotech	1.83	2.03	2.25	2.48	11%
Oekotech	0.68	0.81	0.96	1.14	19%
Total	**417.35**	**462.79**	**513.32**	**569.51**	**11%**

Source: ICRA Baseline Survey report and Wazir Analysis

Chart 1.3: **Value-wise CAGR for Various Technical Textile Segments from 2009-10 to 2012-13**

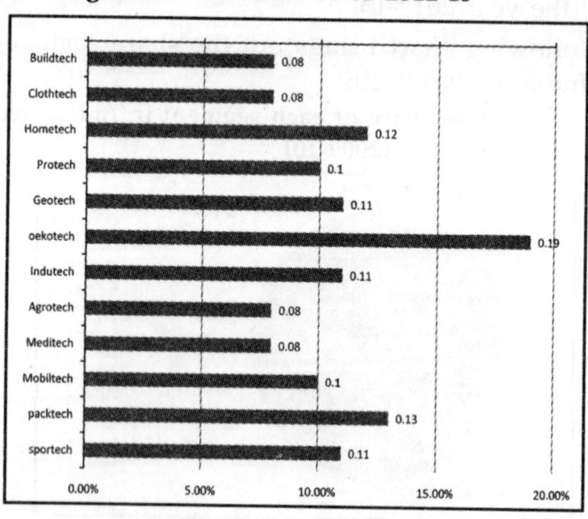

Source: Baseline survey of the Technical Textile industry in India

Overall CAGR is 11%. Packtech, Clothtech and Hometech are the largest segments of the Indian Industry, comprising around 65% of the Indian technical textile market, as evident from the chart. Sportech, Indutech, Geotech, Oekotech, Packtech and Hometech are expected to achieve high growth rates. Though the country consumes products belonging to all 12 categories of technical textiles, the share of indigenous production varies drastically across products. India is a key producer of technical textile products including flexible intermediate bulk containers (FIBCs), tarpaulins, jute carpet backing, hessian, fishnets, surgical dressings, crop covers, etc., which are typically commoditized. The technology-intensive technical textile products such as incontinence diapers, high altitude clothing, etc., are majorly imported with its imports accounting forever 90% of the domestic consumption. The Industry is characterized by the presence of multi-nationals like Ahlstrom, Johnson & Johnson, Du Pont, Procter & Gamble, 3M, SKAPs, Kimberly-Clark, etc., who have set up their manufacturing plants in India, as well as large domestic players like SRF, Entremonde Polycoaters, Kusumgarh Corporates, Supreme Nonwovens, Garware Wall Ropes, Century Enka, Techfab India, Pacific Non Woven, Vardhman, Unimin, etc. The small scale segment also plays a key role, with production of certain goods like canvas tarpaulin, carpet backing, woven sacks, shoe laces, soft luggage, zip fasteners, stuffed toys, fabrication of awnings, canopies and blinds, etc., being concentrated in the small scale.

FUTURE PROJECTIONS

Based on the past growth trends and estimated end user segment growth, it is estimated that the growth rate of Indian Technical Textile Industry over next five years will be about 17% per annum. The segment wise expected growth level is projected .

Table 1.4: Segment wise Expected Growth of Market Size of Indian Technical Textile Industry

Sub Segments	2011-12	2012-13	2013-14	2014-15	2015-16	2016-17	CAGR
Packtech	237.10	284.53	341.43	409.72	491.66	590.00	20%
Clothtech	94.54	110.61	129.42	154.12	177.16	207.28	17%
Hometech	78.31	90.84	105.37	122.23	141.79	164.48	16%
Indutech	48.92	56.25	64.69	74.39	85.55	98.39	15%
Mobiltech	46.89	53.92	62.01	71.32	82.01	94.31	15%
Sportech	42.97	49.41	56.83	65.35	75.15	86.43	15%
Buildtech	29.80	34.28	39.42	45.33	52.13	59.95	15%
Meditech	22.98	26.43	30.40	34.96	40.20	46.23	15%
Protech	18.90	22.12	25.88	30.28	35.42	41.45	17%
Agrotech	7.51	9.01	10.81	12.98	15.57	18.69	20%
Geotech	2.75	3.16	3.64	4.18	4.81	5.53	15%
Oekotech	1.35	1.55	1.78	2.05	2.36	2.71	15%
Total	**632.02**	**742.11**	**871.68**	**1026.91**	**1203.81**	**1415.45**	**17%**

Source: technotex.gov.in/...India's approach to Technical textile-2011 by shri A.B Joshi Textile commissioner; From Textile's Commissioner Office

Chart 1.4: **Market size of Technical Textiles in India**

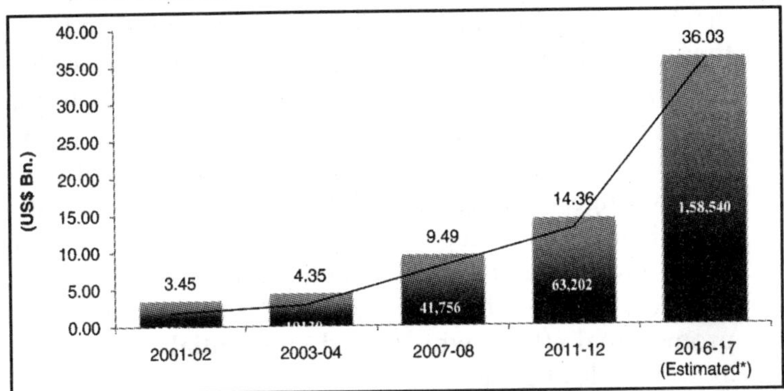

Figures in bar chart are in Rs. crore

* Based on the past trend of growth and estimated end user segment growth, the sub-group on technical textiles for 12th five year plan has projected the market size to Rs. 1,58,540 crore for the year 2016-17 with a growth rate of 20% year on year basis.

Source: (technotex.gov.in/...India's approach to Technical textile-2011 by shri A.B Joshi Textile commissioner)

FACTORS RESPONSIBLE FOR SLOW GROWTH RATE OF TECHNICAL TEXTILE INDUSTRY IN INDIA

India is making a way for gaining a significant place in the global scenario in the technical textiles industry. However it faces a stiff completion from power loom sector. Even in its revival efforts the technical textiles did not find strategic place it deserved. The sector still focuses on modernization of conventional textiles industry. A slow but perceptible sign of growth has been observed in a few specialized fields. There are various factors responsible for the slow growth rate of technical textile industry in India. In order to promote the production of technical textiles, the first and foremost need would be to attract entrepreneurs in the field of technical textiles. Entrepreneurs have so far kept away from the technical textiles in view of the following deterrents:

1. Technical textile and marketing aspects thereof are highly complex. Indian entrepreneurs in textiles have so far not faced this complex situation and therefore have genuine doubts and apprehensions about success in such ventures.

2. Specific technical textiles demand specific raw materials, machinery and equipment, mostly to be imported and therefore, require huge capital towards the project cost.
3. Technical textiles being at an evolving stage in India, generation of technology for product development and establishing specific markets with adequate volumes require huge working capital for a minimum period of 5 years before the entrepreneur could expect fruits of high value addition usually associated with technical textiles. Besides, market development will require sustained promotional efforts which need substantial investments as well as lead time.
4. Developed countries have reached a point of saturation or maturity in bulk of the technical textiles and they are gearing up to enter developing countries including India in a competitive manner in globalized markets. They have the backing of overall experience in various facets of technical textiles and financial muscle, while Indian entrepreneurs have little or no experience in this direction.
5. India being a developing country, the existing norms and mandatory requirements of technical textiles for specific end applications are either outdated or non-existing. As a result, entrepreneurs have an uphill task of introducing technical textiles to end users in the Indian market.
6. Raw material in India is costly, as most of the raw material is needed to be imported from the foreign countries. Attempts should be made to use indigenously available fibers - both natural and manmade, for the technical textile products. On the other hand the growth in industry will provide raw material at cheaper rate as the competitive market would be created.
7. In India little capital is invested in Research & development, consultancy, quality management, testing and evaluation which hold the key to the success of capturing a substantial share of the competitive global market of technical textiles. Accordingly substantial investment in R & D is unavoidable. Strong world class

testing facilities for accurate and relevant evaluation of technical textile must be made available in India to satisfy the stringent and critical requirements of performance related products parameters in the global market. Since most of the technical textiles lose almost their total market value if any of the parameters the parameters fails to confirm to the specifications, the quality control an quality culture should be of a high order to ensure "Right the First Time and Right Every Time".

8. The manpower available in India is not too skilled in their technical and managerial skills. But, India having a large population labor is cheaper so the companies are attracted. Thus the people are needed to be technically trained.
9. So far, little attempt has been made by the Government to boost the market development of technical textiles. For example, there is no legislation for mandatory use of the fire retardant fabrics in high-rise buildings, in public places like exhibitions, cinema halls etc. There is no environmental legislation for the use of Geotextiles and geo-membranes in waste containment for disposal of hazardous wastes as well as for industrial and municipal effluent treatment facilities. Technical developments need support from a regulatory framework based on scientific rationale. For example, airbag technology in automobile is identified as a future prospect in western countries because there is a regulation that new car on road must incorporate airbag technology for the safety of the driver and passengers.
10. Technical textiles sector in India is at a nascent stage in terms of market development. There is lack of awareness amongst the entrepreneurs as well as consumers about the usage, benefits and high growth potential. At present, the major deterrent for expansion of the sector is low demand.
11. There exist duty anomalies in the technical textiles industry wherein an excise duty is levied on the raw material while the finished product has been exempted

from the duty. Some of the products exhibiting such anomaly are – Baby diapers, Incontinence diapers and Sanitary napkins. Anomaly also exists with respect to customs duties. Further, currently, the VAT rate in some states (like Tamil Nadu, Karnataka) is different for the same products based on the base fibre used. There also exists a discrepancy in fiscal treatment of nonwovens and other textile products. Also, DEPB for nonwoven and converted products do not find a mention and needs to be notified.

12. One of the reasons for low penetration of technical textiles, especially in the Meditech segment is the existence of regulations that discourage use of modern technical textile products. For instance, the Indian Drugs & Cosmetics Act 1940 and Indian Pharmacopoeia recognize only woven medical products, due to which the consumption of nonwoven fabrics in medical area is very low. Similarly, in other segments like Geotech, absence of Indian standards has led to a low consumption of geo-textiles over conventional methods. Further, the usage of fire retardant textiles in public places is currently suggested in the National Building Code (NBC) but is not mandatory.
13. Textile industry is concerned over the applicability of GST as the industry involves a lot of inter-state transfers especially at the fabric stage. As GST would be applicable on inter-state depot transfers, it could lead to blockage of funds/cash flow issues as no credit would be available on the finished goods stock at such depots, unless they are sold. The same concern holds for imported goods as well. Another area of concern is the treatment of stock transfers and job work under GST. It is also not clear whether optional cenvat would be available for textile industries under GST.

CONCLUSION

Reasons for the gaining popularity of technical textiles are that they are preferred for their highly specific performance quality. The products are on more scientific lines, technically suitable in producing more durable and convenient end products. They enhance the life and add to the functions of the end products in which they are used. As already discussed above various segments and functions, technical textiles convert the traditional textiles in to more commercial and glorious products.

Another reason that contributes to gaining importance of technical textiles is that industrialized countries being rich in technologies can compete well in terms of innovations and modern productions in comparison to the traditional textiles rich nations which are instead rich in labor and raw material. (Online journal:-TE Textiles Exchange: A Pageant of rich and fascinating Textiles, article: 'Technical Textiles Industry: An Overview) Technical Textiles survive on innovations. Thus, technical textile manufacturers must be ready to invest in research and development and newer equipments too, of which industrialized countries must be capable of. India in order to compete in the global market particularly needs to invest further in general awareness and training of the industrialist and technology development.

REFERENCES

1. Reports of Ministry of Textiles for last Ten years;
2. Reports of Ministry of Commerce and Industry;
3. Reports on Baseline Survey of the Technical Textile industry in India;
4. Reports of Expert Committee on Technical Textiles.

Hometech Industry in India

HOMETECH INDUSTRY

Hometech segment of technical textiles comprises of the textile components used in the domestic environment-interior decoration and furniture, carpeting, protection against the sun, cushion materials, fireproofing, floor and wall coverings, textile reinforced structures/fittings and filter products for vacuum cleaners. They are made of both natural and synthetic fibers.

"Home textiles if are to be praised it can be said that it transforms house into a home. Thus, Home Textile market is recognized as an important part of Technical textiles." (Alexander, 2010, p. 2) Theses products can create comfortable, practical, hygienic and beautiful solutions for modern living. Recent developments in the home furnishings industry include the creation of nonwovens that kill dust mites in bedding, repel dirt and contain antimicrobial qualities. Therefore, "Home textile has become one of the largest technical textile segments comprising household textiles, furnishings and upholstered furniture industry."(Pal, 2010, p. 8) Shanmuga-sundaram (2009) points out that "traditionally textiles have been an important part of the interior of human habitations, as well as human transportation system such as cars, buses, passenger trains, cruise ships or airplanes"(p. 2).In that respect textile served three basic purposes:

- "Decoration (carpets, wall coverings, curtains & drapes, table cloths, etc.);
- Comfort (Upholstery, seat covers, mattresses, bed sheets, blankets, carpets etc.);
- Safety (Safety belts and nets, air bags)." (Shanmugasundaram, 2009, p. 2)

While the basic functions remain unchanged, hometech makes such products more complex, multifunctional or even intelligent by adding various functional properties. Heating, Ventilating and Air-conditioning (HV AC) Filters, filter fabrics, nonwoven wipes, blinds, furniture fabrics and stuff toys are the high growth potential areas. Demand for HVAC filters are driven by the growth of commercial air-conditioning industry on account of continued investments in segments like IT/ITEs, Retail, Entertainment, Pharma, Healthcare, Hospitality, Telecom and Banking. Rising disposable income and changing lifestyle has also driven the demand for stuff toys and nonwoven wipes. Demand for blinds would be driven by increasing construction activity and increasing popularity of blinds.

PRODUCTS/CLASSIFICATION OF HOMETECH

In the global technical textile market, Hometech contributes about 7 percent of the share. However, in India it accounts for about 6 percent of the total technical textile market. (Report of the Expert Committee on Technical Textiles (2004), Vol. 1, Ministry of Textiles, Government of India, New Delhi. p. 111). The technical textile products covered under Hometech are as given below:

1. Fiberfil
2. Carpet backing cloth (Jute & Synthetic)
3. Stuff toys
4. Blinds
5. HV AC filters
6. Filter cloth for vacuum cleaners
7. Mattress and pillow components
8. Nonwoven wipes

9. Mosquito nets
10. Furniture fabrics

AN OVERVIEW OF HOMETECH PRODUCTS

The details of each segment of Hometech is discussed below:

(Final Report on Baseline Survey of the Technical Textile industry in India (2009), March, Office of the Textile Commissioner.

Fiberfil

Fiberfil refers to Polyester Staple Fibers used as filling for pillows, decorative pillows, cushions, bolsters, quilts & comforters, mattresses, mattress toppers, mattress pads, sleeping bags, furniture cushions, furniture backs, insulated garments and soft toys. Traditionally cotton has been used as a filling material in India. Though with rapid development in synthetic fiber production technology special synthetic fibers have been developed as an alternative to cotton for filling purpose.

Market Dynamics and Key Growth Drivers

Fiberfil has to compete with cotton and cotton waste which is the traditional material for filling. Inter fiber competition is a key challenge for the industry. Thus, demand for Fiberfil is significantly impacted by the changes in cotton prices. Moreover, the end consumer of the various products like mattresses, pillows etc is unaware of the benefits of using various kinds of filling material. Thus, initial cost is the key factor in the purchase decision for majority of the customers.

Market Size of Fiberfil

Fiberfil has low penetration in the Indian industry. The installed capacity of Polyester Staple Fiberfil in India is 47400 MT (*Source:* Report on Performance of Chemical & Petrochemical Industry at a Glance, Department of Chemicals & Petrochemicals, Ministry of Chemicals & Fertilizers, Government of India). The production of virgin PSF in 2007-08 was estimated at 42400 MT. As per industry sources the current installed capacity of Regenerated PSF in India is 500 MT/day. Most of these players are operating at a capacity utilization of 50 - 60%.

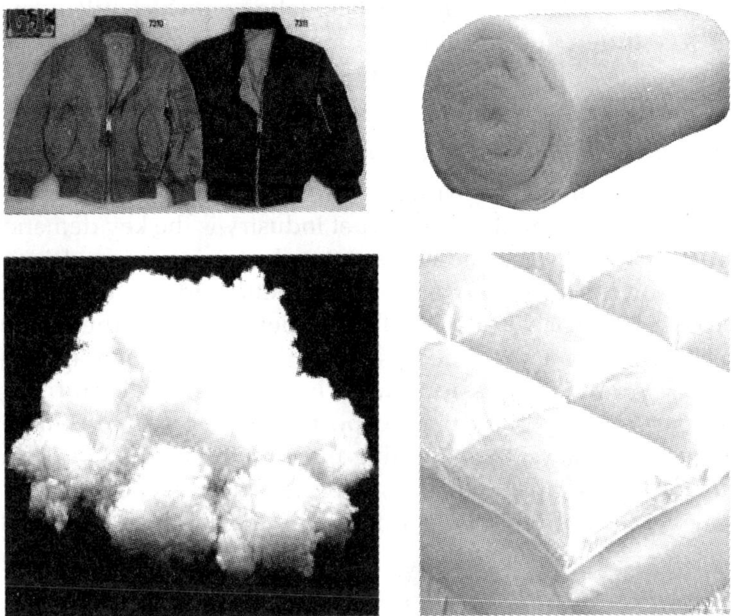

Key Manufacturers

Reliance Industries Limited is the largest manufacturer of Virgin PSF Fiberfil in India. The company markets its product under the brand name Recron. Some other major manufacturers engaged in manufacture of virgin PSF and regenerated PSF are Ganesh Polytex, Arora Fibres limited, Alliance Fibres, Nirmal fibres Private limited.Reliance Industries Ltd. is the largest exporter of Fiberfil. Argentina and USA account for more than 80% of the exports.

Carpet Backing Cloth

A carpet is any loom-woven, felted textile or grass floor covering. The global carpet market for domestic and industrial end use is dominated by several varieties of carpet such as Hand Knotted Carpets, Hand Woven Carpets, Tufted carpets; Needle felt carpets, Flat weave carpets, etc. Carpet Backing Cloth (CBC) is used as the backing material for both woven and tufted carpets as depicted in the figure below: CBC is generally classified into two categories:

- *Primary Carpet backing:* The base fabric on which pile yarns are tufted and anchored to make a carpet;
- *Secondary Carpet backing:* Fabric bonded on the backside of the carpet forming an underlay.

Market Dynamics and Key Growth Drivers

CBC is used as primary and secondary backing for carpets. Thus, growth in the carpet industry is the key demand driver for CBC. The Indian carpet industry is mainly driven by exports. Around 95% of the carpets made in India are exported majorly to USA. The carpet export witnessed a decline in recent years because of rupee appreciation against dollar. As per discussions with industry experts and key industry players the carpet exports are expected to remain stagnant in future, thus, limiting the growth potential of CBC. However, marginal growth is expected in the synthetic CBC only because of replacement of jute by the synthetic category.

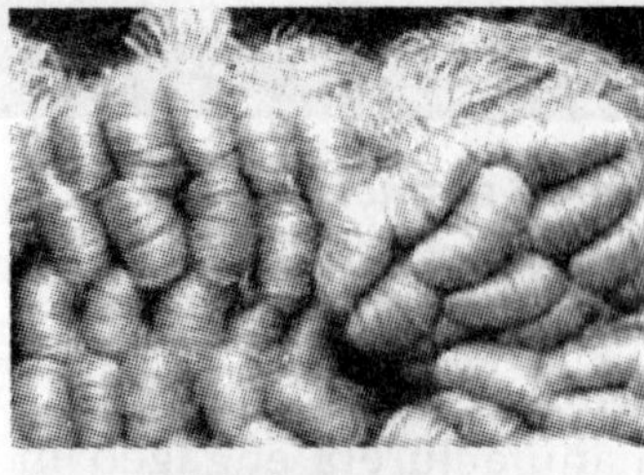

Consumption Pattern and Market Size

CBC is used in majority of the carpets. Since 95% of the carpets manufactured in India are exported, the production of carpets with carpet backing is estimated at 73 million square meters. As per industry sources approximately 10% of the carpets have jute carpet backing. The current market size of jute CBC is estimated at 4750 MT valued at Rs 17 crore. The demand for jute CBC is expected to fall because of its replacement by synthetic CBC.

The market size of synthetic carpet backing cloth is estimated at 128 million sq m valued at Rs. 269 crore. The demand for synthetic carpet backing is expected to increase on account of replacement of jute CBC by synthetic. Key manufacturers of CBC are:

The major manufacturers of Jute CBC are:

- Ludlow Jute
- Birla Corporation
- Gloster Jute

Other players include:

- Auckland International
- Prabartak Jute
- India Jute & Ind
- Champadany Industries Ltd etc. (Capitaline, Annual reports, Company website Industry survey)

Stuffed Toys

Stuffed toys also referred to as plush toys and soft toys are made up of soft knitted fabrics stuffed with filling material. Stuffed toys are popular for a variety of reasons – as toys for kids, as gifts among youngsters, etc.

Market Dynamics and Key Growth Drivers

The young demography, rising disposable income and people's preference for stuffed toys as a gift item augur well for the industry. The industry is seasonal with demand picking up during festive season, Valentine's Day and vacations. The demand is more or less limited to urban area with metros and other big cities accounting for majority of the demand.

Market Size of Stuffed Toys and Future Forecast

Based on interaction with the industry experts and key industry players the domestic market size for stuffed toys is estimated at Rs. 420 crore or 60 million pieces. On account of rising disposable income and increasing preference for stuffed toys amongst both youngsters and kids the stuff toy manufacturers have been witnessing double digit growth rates in the recent years and the industry is expected to grow at a CAGR of 15%. An inflationary increase of 5% is considered for estimating the market size.

Key Manufacturers of Stuffed Toys

The industry is characterized by a few leading players in the organized sector and large number of unorganized home based units. Some of the leading manufacturers are Hanung toys, Sunlord apparels, and Kridnak Udyog. (Industry survey, Hanung annual report). Stuffed toys are mostly manufactured by unorganized home based units. These manufacturers are concentrated in Noida and Kolkata.

Majority of stuffed toys are imported from China. Some soft toys are also imported from France, Singapore, Sri Lanka, Thailand, etc.

Blinds

A window blind is a window covering composed of long strips of fabric or rigid material. A blind limits observation and thus blinds the observer to the view.

Key Growth Drivers

The commercial establishments like offices, hospitals, hotels etc. account for majority of domestic demand for blinds. Vertical blinds are the most popular in offices whereas Roman blinds are used in hotels. Roman blinds are also preferred for farm houses. The growth in domestic demand for blinds is expected to be driven by the infrastructure development planned in the country.

Market Size of Blinds and Future Forecast

As per industry sources the market size for blinds is estimated at Rs 1050 crore. The technical textile component constitutes 60% by value of total blind. Thus, the market size for fabric used in blinds is estimated at Rs 630 crore. The current demand for fabric is estimated at 30 million square meters. Moreover, the penetration of blinds is expected to increase in the domestic market.

Key Manufacturers of Blinds

The fabric and non-fabric components of blinds are manufactured by different producers and finally assembled by one dealer for final installation. The industry has a large number of players in unorganized sector with organized sector accounting for approximately 15% of the total market. The major manufacturers of blinds in the organized sector are:

- Hunter Douglas,
- Mac Décor Ltd.,
- Aerolux India Private Limited and
- Viesta

Various blind manufacturers are only fabricators and do not manufacture fabric. These players do contract manufacturing for production of coated fabrics. There are various players in Uttar Pradesh, Hyderabad, Nasik etc., who manufacture these fabrics. The other players in this industry are Bagga Enterprises, Jain Venetion Blinds Ind., Growrich Horivert Private etc.

HVAC Filters

HVAC stands for heating, ventilating, and air conditioning. The HVAC systems are used in industries, commercial and residential buildings where humidity and temperature need to be closely regulated. The filtration systems in general can be classified as Liquid -Solid separation (e.g. vacuum and pressure filters), Air-Gas separation (e.g. activated carbon filters) and Air-Solid separation (i.e. filters that remove particulate matter from air). HVAC filters belong to the category of air filtration products. The filtration products are also classified based on their end application as depicted:

Market Dynamics and Key Growth Drivers

The demand for HVAC filters is derived from the demand of HVAC systems. The HVAC industry can be broadly classified into the following two segments:

Chart 1: Classification of HVAC Filters

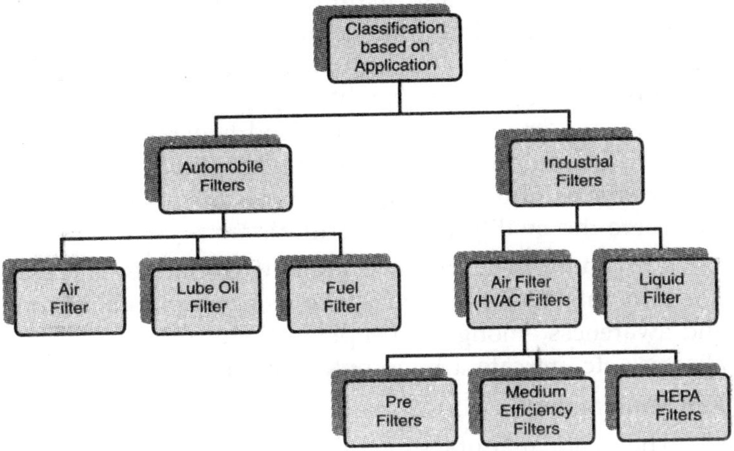

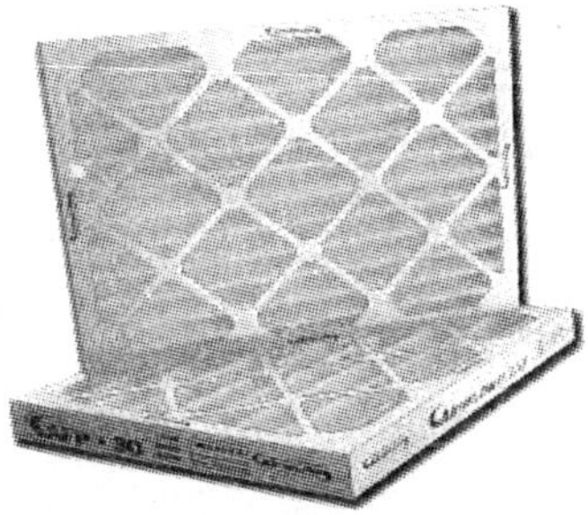

- Classification based on Application
  - Automobile Filters
    - Air Filter
    - Lube Oil Filter
    - Fuel Filter
  - Industrial Filters
    - Air Filter (HVAC Filters
      - Pre Filters
      - Medium Efficiency Filters
      - HEPA Filters
    - Liquid Filter

Split and Window Type Air Conditioners

The type of filter used varies with each manufacturer. Most of the air conditioners use pre filters. The manufacturers have to balance the conflicting objectives of minimizing the power consumption and maintaining the air quality. The demand for centralized air conditioning is derived from various commercial and industrial buildings. Not much attention is given to the quality of air in most cases; cost minimization is the primary goal and hence pre filters are used. HEPA and microvee filters find application in Pharma & Electronics industries, nuclear installations, and hospitals etc where the quality of air is critical.

Air conditioning products are now considered more as a necessity rather than a luxury. The rising disposable incomes and awareness among the people of the respiratory diseases, allergies etc indicate a huge potential for the industry.

Key Manufacturers

The major manufacturers of split and window type air conditioners are LG, Samsung, Videocon, Voltas, Blue star etc. Blue star and Voltas are also the leaders in centralized air conditioning industry with Blue star having a market share of around 30%. Some of the major manufacturers of Air filtration products are:

- Thermadyne Private Limited (Faridabad)
- Spectrum Filtration Pvt. Ltd (Kolkata)
- Anfilco Limited (Gurgaon)
- CRE Industries (Delhi)
- John Fowler (Bangalore)

The filter manufacturers source the filter media from outside. Nonwoven filter media requirement is primarily met by imports. Some of the indigenous manufacturers/suppliers are:

- Dinesh Mills,
- Supreme Nonwoven,
- Mech Tech Industries (Ahmedabad),
- Biyani Industrial Fabrics (Indore)

The filter media is imported from Germany, Netherlands, Taiwan, China and USA. The imports from Netherlands account for around 40% of the imports. The HEPA filters are imported from Malaysia, China, USA, and Netherlands. The exports from India of HVAC filters and filter media are negligible.

Filter Fabrics for Vacuum Cleaners

Vacuum cleaners have a filter to remove the dust from the exhaust air. The dust is collected in a paper bag which can be disposed off. Some of the vacuum cleaners also use HEPA filters.

Market Dynamics and Key Growth Drivers

The demand for vacuum cleaner filters is driven by the demand for vacuum cleaners. The use of vacuum cleaners is mainly concentrated in the urban areas. The demand for vacuum cleaners is triggered by increasing urbanization & disposable incomes, increasing health awareness, unavailability and rising cost of domestic help and increasing number of working women. As per industry sources the demand is also getting a boost because of number of offices and households using carpets which necessitates use of vacuum cleaners.

Market Size of Vacuum Filters and Future Forecast

As per industry sources most of the vacuum cleaners sold in India are imported along with the filter media. The domestic market for vacuum cleaners is estimated to be around 2.6 lakh units per annum which amounts to 33,800 square meters of filter media valued at Rs 35 lakh. The replacement demand of the filter media is also small and these are also reported to be imported. The demand for vacuum cleaners is estimated to have a growth rate of 13% based on the sales trends of Eureka Forbes.

Key Manufacturers

Filter fabrics used in vacuum cleaners are not manufactured by vacuum cleaner manufacturers and are outsourced. The filter fabrics are majorly imported. The import of filter fabric used in vacuum cleaners is negligible. The filter fabric is imported as a part of vacuum cleaners. The exports from India of HVAC filters and filter media are also negligible. Eureka Forbes is the key importer of vacuum cleaners. Filters for vacuum cleaners are imported as a part of vacuum cleaners.

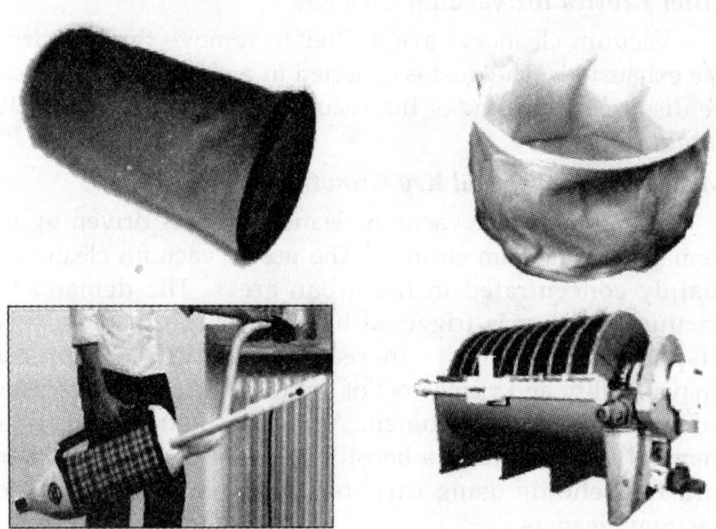

Mattresses and Pillows

A mattress is a mat or pad usually placed on top of bed. Mattresses can be broadly classified as:

- Foam mattresses
- Coir mattresses
- Spring mattresses

Mattresses are made of a filling material like coir, foam etc which provides support to the body. Traditional Indian mattresses are thick quilts made up of cotton stuffing. The protective fabric cover which encases the mattress is called ticking. Ticking fabric holds the filling material in place. It is usually made of cotton and comes in a wide variety of colors and styles. The GSM of the fabric varies from 80 to 200.

Market Dynamics and Key Growth Drivers

The market for mattresses and pillows can be broken down into three segments:

1. Households

2. Hotels
3. Hospitals

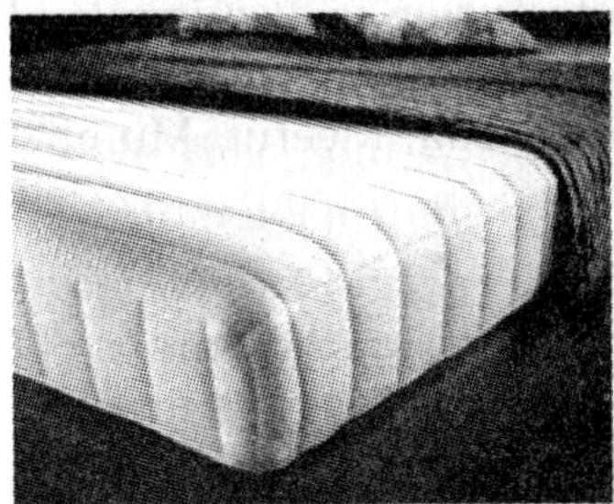

The demand from the household segment accounts for 90-95% of the total market. Mattresses are typically purchased with purchase of a new bed which in turn is dependent on the number of marriages increasing family size etc. As per industry experts mattresses are generally replaced in 8-10 years. Awareness about the pros and cons of different type of mattresses is low, thus, cost plays an important role in the purchasing decision.

Distribution network is a key factor in this industry. Mattresses and pillows are bulky leading to high transportation and warehousing costs. The presence of a number of regional players and relatively less exports and imports are explained by this fact.

Market Size

As per industry sources the demand for all kind of mattresses and pillows is expected to have a moderate growth rate of 3%. An inflationary increase of 5% is considered to estimate the market potential.

Key Manufacturers of the Product

Kurlon Ltd. and Sleepwell are the major manufacturers of mattresses. Kurlon is the market leader with a market share of 40-45% of the organized market. Kurlon is also involved in trading home finishing imported from Taiwan, China, Malaysia, and procured from Ahmadabad, Meerut, Mumbai and Erode.

Nonwoven Wipes

A wipe is a small piece of cloth used for the purpose of cleansing or disinfecting. Wipes could be woven, knitted or nonwoven. Nonwoven wipes have recently gained popularity on account of their excellent absorption and softness. The product is available as dry wipe as well as wet wipe wherein the nonwoven fabric is impregnated with a solution.

Wet wipes are designed for specific application e.g. Baby wipes, Facial wipes, Cleansing wipes, Hand & body wipes, Moist towelettes, Personal hygiene wipes, Feminine hygiene wipes, Antibacterial wipes and Medicated wipes. The usage of baby wipes is well accepted as a convenient, portable, hygienic way to keep babies clean. Antibacterial wipes help to sanitize shopping trolleys, restaurant tables, etc. to reduce the exposure to germs. They also provide an easy way to maintain clean hands more effectively. Personal care wipes are specifically designed to carry cleansing crèmes with specific ingredients to help remove makeup. Wipes also find application in manufacturing and service industries especially in food service and health care. The success of nonwoven wipes is driven by their ease-of-use, disposability, portability and reduced risk of cross-contamination.

Product Characteristics

Non-woven wipes are made from viscose, polyester and polypropylene and are available in variety of sizes ranging from 2 × 5 square cm to 30 × 40 square cm. Majority of nonwoven wipes are manufactured by Spunlace technology. The wipes are expected to have the following properties:

- Smooth and soft texture
- Good absorbance characteristics
- Good moisture retention properties

Market Dynamics and Key Growth Drivers

Busy lifestyle and high disposable income are the key factors for the acceptance of wipes. Wet wipes obviate the need for the use of separate wet and dry combinations in cleaning tasks thus, allowing people to perform daily tasks in substantially less time. Currently the demand for wipes is limited in India but with growing number of middle class families, increasing disposable income and changing lifestyle the demand for wipes is expected to increase in the urban areas. Moreover, product innovations are further likely to boost the demand. Consumption of wipes in foodservice and health care applications is also expected to grow because of heightened health and hygiene concerns.

Key manufacturers of nonwoven wipes:

- Ginni Filaments Ltd.
- Anjani Nonwovens.
- Anjani Udyog Pvt. Ltd.
- Birla Cellulose.
- Aditya Birla group

In addition non woven fabric is imported and converted into wipes in India. Over 50% of the imports take place from China and Singapore. Wipes are also imported from Canada, Germany, USA and UAE. The export of nonwoven wipes is negligible.

Mosquito Nets

The Mosquito net is an essential item used all over the country for protection from mosquitoes; therefore the market of the item exists throughout the year. As other precautions in practice like Mosquito Repellent Mats, Ointment and coils have various side effects; people prefer the use of Mosquito Nets. Therefore the demand is increasing day by day.

Nylon net constitutes around 96% of the raw material cost of the mosquito net. The process of manufacture of Nylon Mosquito Net is very simple. A piece of Net cut in rectangle size as per required size. The required rectangle size Net along with Cotton Tape is spread on sewing Machine and stitch from one corner to the end.

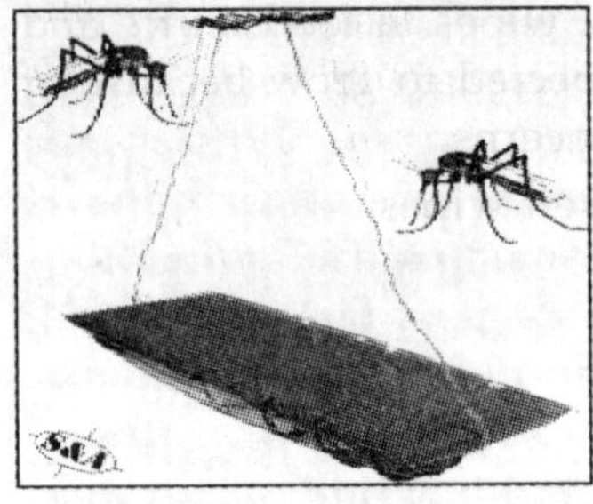

Furniture Fabrics

Indian Furniture industry can be segmented as Home furniture, Office furniture and Contract furniture (majorly the hospitality segment). Fabrics are mainly used in furniture made for seating purposes. Hair, fiber, flock, foam rubber, down, and kapok are used for padding in modern upholstery whereas woven fabrics, plastics, leather and synthetic leather serve as coverings.

Market Dynamics and Key Growth Drivers

Home furniture is the largest segment in the Indian furniture market, accounting for about 65% of the furniture sales. This is followed by the Office furniture segment with a 20% share and the Contract segment with a 15% share.

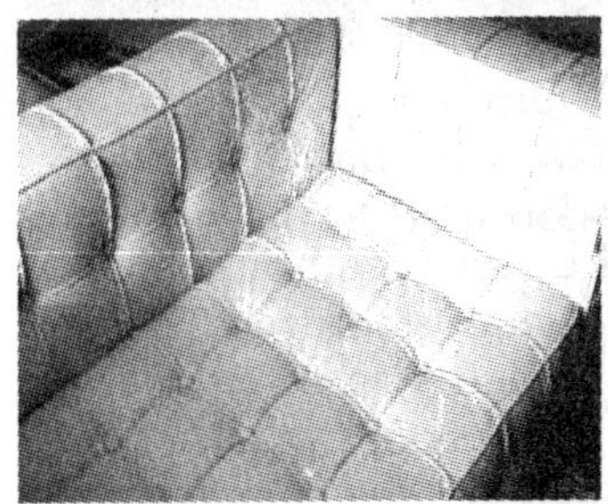

Indigenously manufactured furniture dominates the Indian market with around 62% market share of which upholstered home furniture constitutes 30%.

Wooden furniture comprises the largest share (about 65%) of the furniture in India followed by metal furniture with a 25% share and plastic furniture with a 10% share. Furnishing fabric finds application majorly in the wooden furniture segment.

Steady growth in the Indian economy and the consequent rise in living standard have significantly influenced the Indian furniture industry. The key demand drivers for the industry include changing consumer demographics, real estate/housing boom and growth in tourism/hospitality industry. Increased propensity to spend on lifestyle and consumer products, driven by trends like increase in number of double income families, ease of financing for consumer durables and exposure to global products has also positively impacted the furniture sector. These factors are expected to drive demand for furniture and thus, furniture fabric in the future. Moreover, hotel industry is witnessing an increase in the capacity at a rate of 15% per annum which also augurs well for the industry.

Key Manufacturers of Furniture Fabric

The Flock fabric industry is highly fragmented with most of the firms being sole proprietors/privately held companies. The key players in this segment are:

- The Rishabh V elveleen Limited
- The Girdhar & Company
- Sangam Group of Companies
- Chiripal Group of Companies
- Niranjan DecoFlocks

Artificial leather comprises two major varieties – PU coated and PVC coated fabric. PU coated fabric is majorly imported. PVC coated fabric is manufactured in India, however, the domestic product quality is inferior to the imported fabric thus, leading to imports.

The key players in this segment are:

- Jasch Group NELCO Aman Leather
- Roto Screentech Fenoplast
- Mayur Unicoaters Ltd.
- Veekay Polycoats
- Jay Vinyl
- Jindal Synthetic Leather
- Manish Vinyl Arora Vinyl

Over 90% of artificial leather and around 82% of flock fabric are imported from China. Taiwan has a share of about 5% in the imports of artificial leather followed by Korea, Canada and USA. USA and Belgium are also major suppliers of flock fabric. Over 85% of the velvet fabric is imported from China. Significant imports also take from Italy, Hong Kong and Turkey.

Artificial leather constitutes a major share of the total furnishing fabric exports. UAE accounts for 20% of the total exports followed by Saudi Arabia and USA. Artificial leather is also exported to France, Sri Lanka, Italy and Mozambique.

India also exports significant quantities of velvet fabric and flock fabric. USA accounts for a major share of furniture fabric exports (36% of the total velvet fabric exports and 50% of the total flock fabric exports) of India. Velvet fabric is also exported to UAE, Germany, Italy, Sri Lanka and Turkey. Flock fabric is also exported to UAE, UK, Tanzania, Switzerland and Sri Lanka.

CONCLUSION

Hometech, the third largest segment, accounts for around 12 percent of the technical textiles industry. Hometech includes textiles used in households, particularly for interior decoration and furniture, carpeting, protection against the sun, cushion materials and floor and wall coverings. As per CRISIL Research's estimate, the Hometech industry in India stood at around Rs. 75 billion in 2010-11, with furniture fabric being the largest segment, accounting for a 38 percent share of the industry. Going forward, the growth in this segment will be driven by an increase in the number of addressable households and a simultaneous increase in household income levels. The fastest growing products under the Hometech segment over the next 3 years would be stuffed toys and HAVAC filters. (CRISIL CRB (2012), Sector Focus: Textiles, http://crisil.com/pdf/research/CRISIL-Research-cust-bulletin_jan12.pdf pp. 1-2.).

REFERENCES

1. Reports of Ministry of Textiles for Last Ten Years.
2. Reports of Ministry of Commerce and Industry.
3. Reports on Baseline Survey of the Technical Textile Industry in India.
4. Reports of Expert Committee on Technical Textiles.
5. Specialty Fibre - Section VII, Ministry of Textiles, Government of India, p. 530, retrieved from www.texmin.nic.in/policy/fiber_policy_main.htm
6. Technical Textiles in India – Current a Future Market Scenario Retrieved from www.imacs.in/.../technical%20textiles%20in%20india%20-... pp.11-12

7. http://technotex.gov.in/hometech.html
8. Final Report on Baseline Survey of the Technical Textile Industry in India (2009), March, Office of the Textile Commissioner http://technotex.gov. in/Revised_Final_Report_Baseline_Survey_of_Technical_Textile%20industry_in_India.pdf, pp. 40-42.
9. Final Report on Baseline Survey of the Technical Textile Industry in India (2009), March, Office of the Textile Commissioner http://technotex.gov.in/Revised_Final_Report_Base line_Survey_of_Technical_Textile%20industry_in_India.pdf, pp.381-420.
10. Best Practice Guide: Technical Textiles and Composite Manufacturing, National Composite Network, Retrieved form www.compositesuk.co.uk/LinkClick.aspx? fileticket...tabid=111
11. David Rigby Associates: Technical Textiles and Nonwovens: World Market Forecasts to 2010 Retrieved from www.davidrigbyassociates.com
12. Technical Textiles in India – Current a Future Market Scenario Retrieved from www.imacs.in/.../technical%20textiles%20in%20india%20-... pp. 11-12.
13. Final Report on Baseline Survey of the Technical Textile Industry in India (2009), March, Office of the Textile Commissioner.
14. Report of the Expert Committee on Technical Textiles (2004), Vol. 1, Ministry of Textiles, Government of India, New Delhi. p. 111. http://technotex.gov.in/Revised_Final_Report_Baseline_Survey_of_Technical_Textile%20industry_in_India.pdf, pp. 601-603.
15. Final Report on Baseline Survey of the Technical Textile Industry in India (2009), March, Office of the Textile Commissioner http://technotex.gov.in/Revised_Final_Report_Base line_Survey_of_Technical_Textile%20industry_in_India.pdf, pp.613-614.
16. Final Report on Baseline Survey of the Technical Textile Industry in India (2009), March, Office of the Textile Commissioner http://technotex.gov.in/Revised_Final_Report_ Baseline_Survey_of_Technical_Textile%20industry_in_India.pdf, p. 44.
17. Final Report on Baseline Survey of the Technical Textile Industry in India (2009), March, Office of the Textile Commissioner http://technotex.gov.in/Revised_Final_Report_Baseline_Survey_of_Technical_Textile%20industry_in_India.pdf, pp.379-380.
18. CRISIL CRB (2012), Sector Focus: Textiles, http:// crisil.com/ pdf/ research/ CRISIL-Research-cust-bulletin_jan12.pdf pp. 1-2.

Growth of the Hometech Industry in India

HOMETECH TEXTILES: GLOBAL OVERVIEW

The markets for most traditional Hometech products such as carpets, furnishing fabrics and mattresses are fairly mature in Western economies. However, as disposable incomes have increased and the relatively wealthy middle classes have grown in number in many developing countries, the growth in the market for home textiles has already accelerated. This has in turn promoted the expansion of local manufacturing both for the finished products and for the supporting Hometech supply chains.

India and China have demonstrated the highest growth rates of Hometech technical textiles over recent years and are forecast to continue to grow at about 5% per annum in the short term. This trend will be further boosted by the increasing globalization of the industry as standards and styles have already begun to popularize more internationally.

This has lead to increased trade opportunities for low cost suppliers into the more developed markets, and has also created opportunities for established manufacturers in the West to expand their export business into the developing markets.

The demand for many products in the Hometech application area fluctuates broadly in line with the economic cycle, but with more severe peaks and troughs. Firstly, many end products in this sector (such as beds, upholstered furniture and carpets) represent 'big ticket' consumer purchases that are easily deferrable. As a result, end product demand is more highly variable than most other end-use segments. Secondly, purchases of household textiles are closely related to the highly cyclical housing market. Thirdly, contract (i.e. non-domestic) demand is closely linked with the fluctuating level of activity in infrastructure development, construction and capital spending.

Final Report on Baseline Survey of the Technical Textile industry in India (2009), March, Office of the Textile Commissioner.

In the past years the Hometech industry has been witnessing tremendous growth. At global level of the total technical textile market, Hometech contributes about 7 percent of the share and the industry is expected to be dominated by technical application of various textile materials in different forms in the next millennium. Global demand for Hometech textiles has led to increased investment in Indian technical textile industry (David Rigby Associates, 2010).

The following Table exhibits the global market size of Hometech textiles from the year 2000 to 2012 which was estimated by David Rigby Associates, International Consultants who are the only agency following technical textiles.

Table 3.1: Global Market Size of Hometech Textiles (2000-12)

Years	Volume (000 Tonnes)	Value (US $ million)
2000	2186	6750
2005	2499	7622
2007	2634	8086
2010	2853	8778
2012	3009.1	9006.3
CAGR (%)	2.7	2.66

Source: David Rigby Associates. (2010). Technical Textiles and Non wovens: World market forecasts to 2010. Retrieved February 4, 2012, from http://www.fibre2fashion.com/industry-article/pdffiles/Technical-Textiles-and-Nonwovens.pdf. p. 8.

Table 3.1 shows an average annual world-wide growth in volume terms at the rate of 2.7 percent during the period 2000 to 2012 and in terms of value the growth has been @2.66% in US $ million.

The increase in the market size also reflects the increase in the consumption levels of the Hometech products. The following Table 3.2 shows the rise in end-use consumption of Hometech textiles in various regions like North America, South America, Western Europe, Eastern Europe, South Asia, North East Asia, South East Asia and rest of the World. It gives an analysis of Hometech textiles by region from year 1995 to 2010 with CAGR (%).

The world consumption of Hometech textiles from year 1995 to 2010 has increased significantly as per given in above table 4.2. In the year 1995, the consumption for Hometech textiles was estimated to have a volume of 1863.6 tones which increased to 2185.9 tones during 2000 with a CAGR of 3.2% and further to 2498.6 tones with a CAGR of 2.7% in 2005. In 2010, the consumption was at 2853.1 tones with the same CAGR of 2.7%.

The chart 3.1 reveals that the major consumers of the Hometech products are America, followed by British and Asia. Over 42.58% of consumption was found in North and South America followed by Western and Eastern Europe with a share of 32.2% and South Asia, North East Asia and South East Asia together representing a share of 20% while rest of the world constitutes a share of 5.7% only.

INTERNATIONAL TRADE OF INDIAN HOMETECH INDUSTRY

In India the Hometech industry has shown a substantial improvement. There has been an increase in the demand and consumption of the Hometech products in the country. This in turn has given a boost to the production, imports exports of the industry products. This can be judged by the data represented below. The following table represents the production, export, import and trade balance of Hometech industry in India to the rest of the world from 2002-03 to 2011-12.

Table 3.2: World Hometech Consumption, 1995-2010, by Region in Volume Terms (000 Tonnes)

Region	Year												CAGR (%)		
	1995	2000	2001	2002	2003	2004	2005	2006	2007	2008	2009	2010	95-00	00-05	05-10
North America	801.8	903.6	911.9	917.4	950.4	983.6	1018.9	1040.2	1057.8	1075.2	1092.4	1109.9	2.4	2.4	1.7
South America	53.3	66	67.3	68.8	72.5	76.7	80.9	85.5	90.1	95	99.9	105.1	4.4	4.2	5.4
Western Europe	553.1	675.9	692	703.4	719.3	738.7	758.7	774.8	791	807.1	823	839.3	4.1	2.3	2
Eastern Europe	35.6	40.5	42.2	44.2	46.5	48.9	51.4	54.8	58.3	62	65.9	70.1	2.6	4.9	6.4
South Asia	34.8	50.4	53.6	57.1	61.6	66.4	71.4	77.2	83.4	89.9	96.8	104.2	7.7	7.2	7.9
North East Asia	234.8	284.3	289	293	303.3	314.6	326.7	338.5	351.5	365.1	379.2	394.1	3.9	2.8	3.8
South East Asia	28.8	37.5	38.8	40.3	43	45.8	49	52.3	55.9	59.7	63.6	67.7	5.4	5.5	6.7
Rest of the World	121.3	127.7	129.3	131.5	134.6	138.1	141.6	145.5	149.5	153.7	158.1	162.8	1	2.1	2.8
Total	**1863.6**	**2185.9**	**2224**	**2255.7**	**2331.2**	**2412.7**	**2498.6**	**2568.7**	**2637.6**	**2707.7**	**2778.9**	**2853.1**	**3.2**	**2.7**	**2.7**

Source: David Rigby Associates. (Personal Communication, 2003).HOMETECH: Technical components for Furniture, interior textiles and floor coverings.

The following Chart 3.1 represents the consumption of Hometech textiles in 2010 by region (%):

Chart 3.1: **End-use Consumption of Hometech Textiles in 2010, by Region (%)**

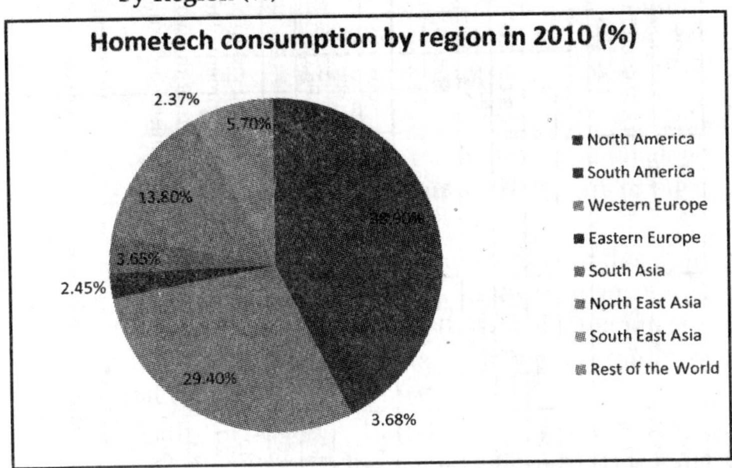

Source: David Rigby Associates. (Personal Communication, 2003). HOMETECH: Technical components for Furniture, interior textiles and floor coverings.

Trade of Indian Hometech Industry with the Rest of the World

Data noted in the following table 3.3 presents the Production, Export, Import and Trade balance of Indian Hometech industry to the rest of the world as a whole and measures their growth rates on the basis of previous year during 2002-2012:

From the table 3.3 we observe that the production has gone up from 883.39 Cr. in 2002-03 to 7831 Cr. in2011-2012 i.e a sharp increase in the past ten years. The percentage increase remained constant in the first few years but production jumped up by 61.64% in the year 2011-12 from 2010-2011.

A big leap in the import can also be observed in the first two years where it has gone up by 135.63 % in the year 2003-04 from the year 2002-03. Though import grew in the later years consistently but from 2010 to 2012 there was a substantial increase by 41.97%.

Table 3.3: Production, Export, Import and Trade balance and their Growth (%) from 2002 to 2012

Years	Production (Values in Rs. Cr.)	Production (Growth (%)	Export (Values in Rs. Cr.)	Export Growth (%)	Import (Values in Rs. Cr.)	Import Growth (%)	Trade Balance (Values in Rs. Cr.)	Trade Balance Growth (%)
2002-03	883.39		146.52		165.52		-19	
2003-04	1029.72	16.56	1542.91	953.04	390.01	135.63	1152.9	-6167.89
2004-05	1199.77	16.51	2015.85	30.65	529.17	35.68	1486.68	28.95
2005-06	1397.89	16.51	1106.69	-45.10	782.16	47.81	324.53	-78.17
2006-07	1628.74	16.51	2578.16	132.96	1070.02	36.80	1508.14	364.72
2007-08	5025.00	208.52	2712.05	5.19	1346.22	25.81	1365.83	-9.44
2008-09	3797.52	-24.43	2294.63	-15.39	1732.84	28.72	561.79	-58.87
2009-10	4321.10	13.79	2114.83	-7.84	1825.32	5.34	289.51	-48.47
2010-11	4844.68	12.12	2540.84	20.14	2444.82	33.94	96.02	-66.83
2011-12	7831.00	61.64	3299.54	29.86	3470.80	41.97	-171.26	-278.36

Source: (1) Production Data from 2002-03 to 2007-08:Ministry of Textiles. (2006). Report of the working group on Textiles & Jute industry for the Eleventh Five year plan (2007-12).New Delhi: Ministry of Textiles, Government of India. p. cxvi.

(2) Production Data for the years 2007-08 and 2011-12:Ministry of Textiles. (2011). Report of the working group on Textiles & Jute industry for twelfth five year plan (2012-17), Chapter 16. New Delhi: Ministry of Textiles, Government of India. p. 265.

(3) Production Data for the years 2008-09, 2009-10 and 2010-11 have been calculated by the researcher using interpolation

(4) Export and Import: Government of India, Ministry of Commerce and Industry, Department of Commerce, Country – wise Export Import Data Bank.

This rate of growth in both production and consumption reflects an improvement in consumption of Hometech Products too.

Similarly the exports grew up sharply from 146.52 Cr. in 2002-03 to 3299.54 Cr. in 2011-12. In terms of rate of growth there was a big jump from 2002-03 to 2003-04 i.e. by 953.04% but gradually it slowed down. It can be seen that in some of the year's growth was even negative but in the last years it went up by 29.86%. On the other hand on analyzing the trade balance of the industry it is found that though it was positive in the former years but later remained negative continuously in the last six years. It may be drawn that figures of imports always remained bigger than exports.

The figures represent a substantial improvement in overall performance of the industry. The above data can be represented with the help of following charts:

Chart 3.2: **Production, Export, Import and Trade balance of Hometech industry (2002-12)**

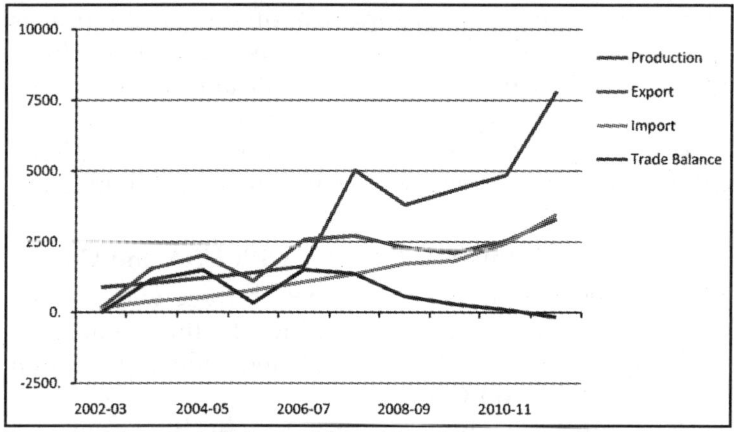

Source: Developed on the basis of data given above

Value-wise around 13% of the total consumption is imported. As per volume, 67% of HVAC filters consumed are imported whereas the value-wise import of nonwoven wipes is 80% of the total consumption. Majority of imports are from Germany and Netherland (HVAC filters) and China. Majority of wipes are imported from China and Singapore.

Chart 3.3: **Growth of production, export, import and trade balance of Homtech industry in the past decade**

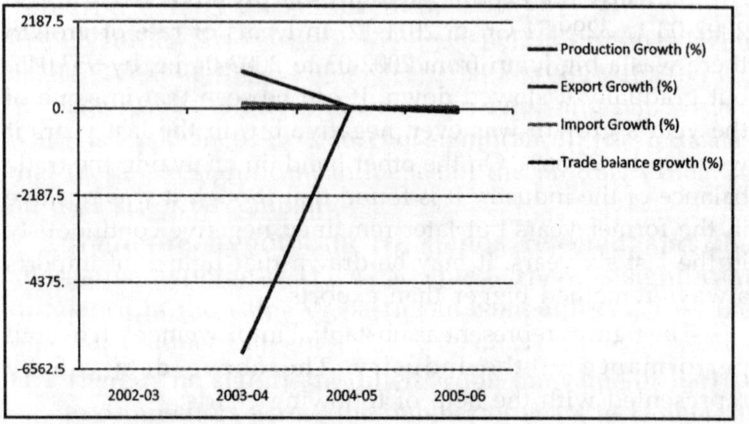

Source: Developed on the basis of data given above.

The exports in the Hometech segment are not very significant; value-wise around 6% of the production is exported. Fiberfil, which exports 9% of its production volume and furniture fabrics, which exports about 14% of its production value are the only products with significant export. The key export markets are the US and Argentina. (Final Report on Baseline Survey of the Technical Textile industry in India (2009).

Trade of Indian Hometech Industry with USA and China

After analyzing the Indian Hometech trade with the rest of the world, the researcher proceeded further to analyze the Indian Hometech trade with USA and China. The reason for choosing USA and China are:

1. USA is the largest trading partner of India. India's biggest export market for textiles products is USA. As per report of the Ministry of textiles India exported 17.21% of its textiles to US market in the year 2011-12. It is followed by China which accounts for 10.37% in 2011-12 of the total textiles exports. From the same source it was found that India is importing largest part of textiles from Chine i.e. 42.31% followed by USA 5.64% in the year 2011-12.

(Source: DGCIS, Updated on 01.03.2013). Thus it becomes necessary to study the growth of Hometech exports and imports with these countries.

2. Another reason for taking China for analysis is that China is the strongest competitor of India. The researcher aims to check out whether with its strongest competitor the Hometech trade improved in the past years or not. If yes, then to what extent?

The following table gives exports of Indian Hometech Product to USA and China.

Table 3.4: Exports of Hometech Products to USA and China

(Values in Rs. Lakhs)

Years	USA	Growth (%)	China	Growth (%)
2002-03	3,691.17		324.98	
2003-04	56,222.54	1423.16	303.24	-6.69
2004-05	66,386.00	18.08	2,281.05	652.23
2005-06	87,254.60	31.44	497.88	-78.17
2006-07	67,685.88	-22.43	5,651.36	1035.08
2007-08	66,054.29	-2.41	2,029.28	-64.09
2008-09	49,290.91	-25.38	1,185.03	-41.60
2009-10	33,582.32	-31.87	608.46	-48.65
2010-11	50,129.28	49.27	1,000.13	64.37
2011-12	58,881.54	17.46	2,039.47	103.92
Total	**539,178.53**		**15920.88**	

Source: Government of India, Ministry of Commerce and Industry, Department of Commerce, Country - wise Export Import Data Bank.

From table and graph above it can be concluded that there was a substantial increase in the exports of the Hometech products to USA from the year 2002 to 2008. But from 2008-2010 it dipped down but gradually recovered 2010 onwards. Fall down in the exports was due to various reasons such as appreciation of rupees in 2008 and looming recession in USA in those years.

Chart 3.4: **Exports of Hometech Products to USA and China**

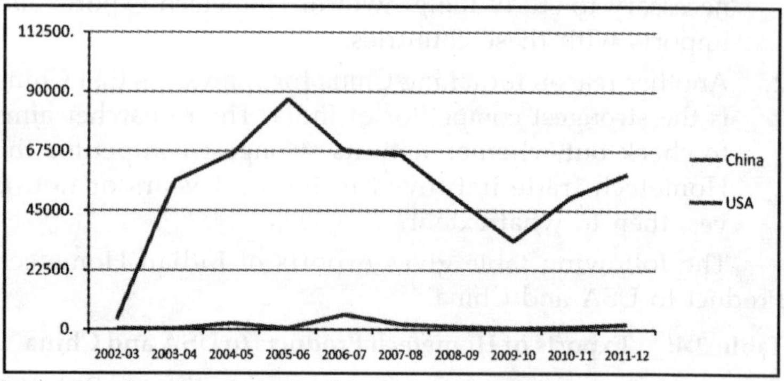

Source: Developed on the basis of data given above

On the other hand not much improvement can be observed in Hometech exports to China. Highest could be seen in the year 2006-07 but gradually it dipped down within years. In last ten years the exports to China remained almost constant. The most important reason for this is that the Hometech industry is already strongly established in the country because of which it is in a position to export considerably to the world and India in particular. This is proved in the data collected below.

The table below represents the data of imports of Hometech products in to India from USA and China:

Table 3.5: Imports of Hometech Products from USA and China

(Values in Rs. Lakhs)

Years	USA	Growth (%)	China	Growth (%)
2002-03	508.07		2,985.93	
2003-04	2,009.41	295.50	10,421.08	249.01
2004-05	2,394.92	19.19	18,997.98	82.30
2005-06	2,485.71	3.79	41,699.13	119.49
2006-07	3,052.50	22.80	61,869.95	48.37
2007-08	3,840.44	25.81	78,998.86	27.69
2008-09	7,755.16	101.93	106,901.75	35.32
2009-10	10,010.12	29.08	115,640.52	8.17
2010-11	8,803.31	-12.06	159,878.13	38.25
2011-12	12,151.46	38.03	241,660.97	51.15
Total	**53,011.10**		**839,054.30**	

Source: Government of India, Ministry of Commerce and Industry, Department of Commerce, Country - wise Export Import Data Bank.

Chart 3.5: **Imports of Hometech Products from USA and China**

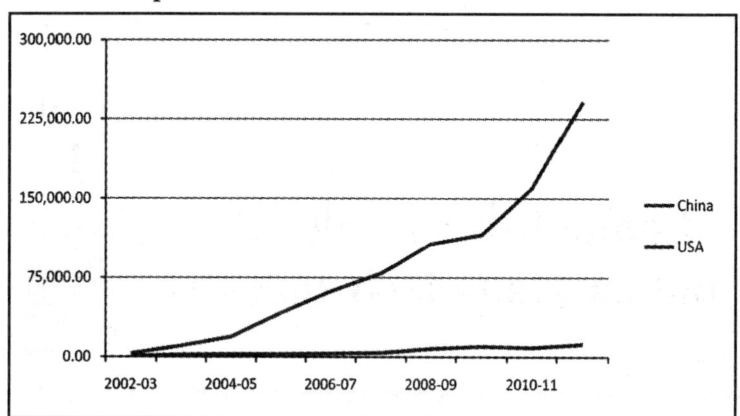

Source: Developed on the basis of data given above

From the data and the graph regarding imports from USA and China we may conclude that the picture is reverse to that of exports. In the past decade the imports from China has substantially increased. The increase has been sharper since 2007-08 onwards. Where as on the other hand not much fluctuation or rather improvement can be observed in imports from USA. This indicates that for Indian Hometech importers China is better in terms of trade and price.

CONCLUSION

After analyzing the consumption and international trade of Indian Hometech industry with the world in general and USA and China in particular, it may be concluded that the industry in India is growing substantially to meet the demand. This can be witnessed by the improvement in production. In spite of the growth and improvement in the Indian Hometech industry we find that it still lags behind in the international market. The industry needs to grow stronger to come at par with its competitors. In order to study the industry further i.e. its strengths and weaknesses, researcher conducted the competitive analysis of the industry by applying Porter's five forces model. The next chapter explains the concept and application of the model.

CHAPTER 4

Competitive Analysis of Indian Hometech Industry

INTRODUCTION

After exploring the Hometech industry and understanding its place in the global market, it becomes necessary to study its competitive strength. Indian Hometech Industry is in nascent stage and needs to establish itself more firmly. Any business happens in highly complex and competitive environment. It's important to understand strengths and weaknesses of its current and potential competitors. This makes it very important for startups to understand and analyze their competitors and frame their growth strategies [both offensive and defensive] accordingly. In order to grow and develop it becomes necessary to understand the competitors thoroughly and it becomes impertinent that one does a systematic analysis and assessment rather than relying on informal knowledge and chunks of data that one might 'know'. The most influential and analytical model for assessing the nature of competition in the industry is Micheal Porter's Five Forces model. This model is used to analyse the competitive strength of the Indian Hometech Industry.

PORTER'S FIVE COMPETITIVE FORCES: A MODEL FOR INDUSTRY ANALYSIS

The Porter's Five Forces tool is a simple but powerful tool for understanding where power lies in a business situation. This is useful, because it helps you understand both the strength of your business and current competitors.

Michael Porter's five forces is a model used to explore the environment in which a product or company operates to generate competitive advantage. Five forces analysis looks at five key areas mainly the threat of entry, the power of buyers, the power of suppliers, the threat of substitutes, and competitive rivalry (advantage).

The model of the Five Competitive Forces was developed by Michael E. Porter in his book "Competitive Strategy: Techniques for Analyzing Industries and Competitors" in 1980. Since that time the 'five forces tool' has become an important method for analyzing an organisation's industry structure in strategic processes.

Michael Porter's model is based on the insight that a corporate strategy should meet the opportunities and threats in the organisations external environment. Especially, competitive strategy should base on an understanding of industry structures and the way they change. Porter has identified five competitive forces that shape every industry and every market. These forces determine the intensity of competition and hence the profitability and attractiveness of an industry. The objective of corporate strategy should be to modify these competitive forces in a way that improves the position of the organisation. Porter's model supports analysis of the driving forces in an industry. Based on the information derived from the Five Forces Analysis, management can decide how to influence or to exploit particular characteristics of their industry. ("Porter's Five Forces", 2012)

THE STUDY

Understanding the importance of the emerging industry and the Michael E. Porter's five forces model, research work proceeds to explore the Hometech industry with the help of this model. Efforts are been made to penetrate deeper in to the industry and study its competitive strength by using the Michael E Porter's - 'Five Forces' Model. The five forces are:

1. Bargaining power of suppliers;
2. Bargaining power of buyers
3. Threat to new entrants;
4. Threat of substitutes products or services; and
5. Rivalry among existing firms.

These forces are verified across different segments of the home tech industry.

The present study has been carried out on the micro-level using quantitative as well as qualitative approach to the research. This micro study is undertaken to examine the competitiveness of the Hometech industry. The study shall reveal the inherent strength and weaknesses existing and available opportunities and threats for the industry. In order to accomplish this, a well structured questionnaire was designed and got filled from the respondents across the industry (producers and exporters).

HYPOTHESES OF THE STUDY

Hypotheses are formulated on the basis of porter's five forces model to determine the competitiveness of the Hometech Industry along with the categories available. The Porter's five forces i.e. Bargaining power of suppliers, Bargaining power of buyers, Threat to new entrants, Threat of substitutes products or services and Rivalry among existing firms have been taken as variables to measure the competitive strengths of the Hometech Industry. These variables are measured across:

1. Different product categories existing in Hometech industry; and
2. The number of years for which a firm is running in their business.

Hometech segment of technical textiles comprises of the textile components, classified as:

(a) Fiberfil

(b) Carpet backing cloth (Jute & Synthetic)
(c) Stuff toys
(d) Blinds
(e) HVAC filters
(f) Filter cloth for vacuum cleaners
(g) Mattress and pillow components
(h) Nonwoven wipes
(i) Mosquito nets
(j) Furniture fabrics

For the purpose of data collection and analysis these have been regrouped in to five categories given as follows:

Table 4.1: Product Category

(a)	Category 1	Carpet backing cloth (Jute & Synthetic) and Mosquito nets.
(b)	Category 2	Blinds and Furniture fabrics.
(c)	Category 3	Fiberfil, pillow components and Stuff toys.
(d)	Category 4	Mattress and Nonwoven wipes.
(e)	Category 5	HVAC filters Filter cloth for vacuum cleaners.

On the basis of this framework, following hypotheses have been framed:

H_{01}: There is no significant difference in the value of bargaining power of suppliers across the Product Category in Hometech industry.

H_{02}: There is no significant difference in the value of bargaining power of suppliers across the number of years in Hometech industry.

H_{03}: There is no significant difference in the value of bargaining power of buyers across the Product Category in Hometech industry.

H_{04}: There is no significant difference in the value of bargaining power of buyers across the number of years in Hometech industry.

H_{05}: There is no significant difference in the value of barriers to new entrants across the Product Category in Hometech industry.

H_{06}: There is no significant difference in the value of Barrier to new entrants across the number of years in Hometech industry.

H_{07}: There is no significant difference in the value of Barrier to substitutes across the Product Category in Hometech industry.

H_{08}: There is no significant difference in the value of Barrier to substitutes across the number of years in Hometech industry.

H_{09}: There is no significant difference in the value of Barrier to competitors across the Product Category in Hometech industry.

H_{10}: There is no significant difference in the value of Barrier to competitors across the number of years in Hometech industry.

TESTING OF HYPOTHESIS: ANALYSIS

The primary data being collected have been put to statistical tests to deduce the results. After statistically applying the data is analysed, followed by the interpretations:

Data Analysis

(a) ***Bargaining power of the suppliers with reference to Product Category and number of years in Hometech industry.***

H_{01}: There is no significant difference in the value of bargaining power of suppliers across the Product Category in Hometech industry.

Table 4.2: Bargaining Power of Suppliers with Product Category

Product Category	N	Mean	Std. Deviation	F	Sig.
Category 1 (Carpet backing cloth (Jute & Synthetic) and Mosquito nets.)	6	3.4444	.96225	3.238	0.038
Category 2 (Blinds and Furniture fabrics)	12	4.0952	.49868		
Category 3 (Fiberfil, pillow components and Stuff toys.)	6	2.7778	.38490		
Category 4 (Mattress and Nonwoven wipes)	6	3.5556	.50918		
Category 5 (HVAC filters Filter cloth for vacuum cleaners.)	6	3.3333	.51640		
Total	**36**	**3.5455**	**.67882**		

In order to determine the variation in the responses of manufacturers across the Product Category on bargaining power of suppliers One Way ANOVA is used.

The table above shows the mean value obtained on bargaining power of the suppliers across the Product Category manufactured by the Hometech manufacturers.

This has been observed that the manufacturers of blinds and furniture fabrics obtained the highest mean value on bargaining power of the suppliers. However, those units manufacturing the fibrefill, pillow components and Stuff toys stand at the minimum mean value of the bargaining power.

The results of ANOVA shows F= 3.238 and Sig. = .038, which is less than .05 (95% level of significance). This indicates that there exists a significant difference in the value of bargaining power of the suppliers across the Product Category.

Therefore hypothesis H_{01} stands rejected and the alternative hypothesis H_{01a} is accepted. There is significant difference in the value of bargaining power of suppliers across the Product Category.

H_{02}: There is no significant difference in the value of bargaining power of suppliers across the number of years in Hometech industry.

Table 4.3: Bargaining Power of Suppliers Across the Number of Years

No. of Years	N	Mean	Std. Deviation	F	Sig
0-5 yrs.	4	4.0000	.00000	1.783	0.186
5-10 yrs.	6	3.4444	1.01835		
10-15 yrs.	9	3.9444	.49065		
>15 yrs.	17	3.2727	.64667		
Total	**36**	**3.5455**	**.67882**		

The result of the test shows the mean value obtained on bargaining power of the suppliers across the number of years of business by the Hometech manufacturers.

The statistics shows that the manufacturers in this industry since more than 15 years obtained the lowest mean value on bargaining power of the suppliers. However, those units manufacturing for less than 5 years stand at the maximum mean value of the bargaining power.

The results of ANOVA shows F= 1.783 and Sig. = .186, which is more than .05 (95% level of significance). This indicates that there is no significant difference in the value of bargaining power of the suppliers across the speciality material.

Therefore hypothesis H_{01} stands accepted and the alternative hypothesis H_{01a} is rejected. There is no significant difference in the value of bargaining power of suppliers across the number of years.

(b) ***Bargaining power of the buyers with reference to Product Category and number of years.***

H_{03}: There is no significant difference in the value of bargaining power of buyers across the Product Category in Hometech industry.

Table 4.4: Bargaining Power of Buyers with Product Category

Product Category	N	Mean	Std. Deviation	F	Sig.
Category 1 (Carpet backing cloth (Jute & Synthetic) and Mosquito nets.)	5	2.5833	.14434		
Category 2 (Blinds and Furniture fabrics)	12	2.8929	.34932		
Category 3 (Fiberfil, pillow components and Stuff toys.)	6	3.0833	.14434	0.692	0.608
Category 4 (Mattress and Nonwoven wipes)	4	2.9167	.72169		
Category 5 (HVAC filters Filter cloth for vacuum cleaners.)	9	3.0417	.51031		
Total	**36**	**2.9205**	**.41823**		

The result of the test shows the mean value obtained on bargaining power of the buyers across the Product Category manufactured by the Hometech manufacturers.

The statistics shows that the manufacturers of toys and fillings obtained the highest mean value on bargaining power of the buyers. However, those units manufacturing the floor coverings stand at the minimum mean value of the bargaining power of the buyers.

The results of ANOVA shows F= .692 and Sig. = .608, which is more than .05 (95% level of significance). This indicates that there exists no significant difference in the value of bargaining power of the buyers across the Product Category.

Therefore hypothesis H_{01}stands accepted and the alternative hypothesis H_{01a} is rejected. There is no significant difference in the value of bargaining power of buyers across the Product Category.

H_{04}: There is no significant difference in the value of bargaining power of buyers across the number of years in Hometech industry.

Table 4.5: Bargaining Power of Buyers Across the Number of Years

No. of Years	N	Mean	Std. Deviation	F	Sig.
0-5 yrs.	4	2.6250	.17678	3.149	0.051
5-10 yrs.	6	2.6667	.28868		
10-15 yrs.	8	2.7083	.24580		
>15 yrs.	18	3.1591	.43693		
Total	**36**	**2.9205**	**.41823**		

The result of the test shows the mean value obtained on bargaining power of the buyers across the number of years of business by the Hometech manufacturers.

The statistics shows that the firms in this industry since more than 15 years obtained the highest mean value on bargaining power of the buyers. However, those firms for less than 5 years stand at the minimum mean value of the bargaining power.

The results of ANOVA shows F= 3.149 and Sig. = .051, which is equal to .05 (95% level of significance). This indicates that there is no significant difference in the value of bargaining power of the buyers across the speciality material.

Therefore hypothesis H_{01} stands accepted and the alternative hypothesis H_{01a} is rejected. There is no significant difference in the value of bargaining power of buyers across the number of years.

(c) ***Barrier to new entrants with reference to Product Category and number of years.***

H_{05}: There is no significant difference in the value of barriers to new entrants across the types of Product Category in Hometech industry.

Table 4.6: Barrier to New Entrants with Product Category

Product Category	N	Mean	Std. Deviation	F	Sig.
Category 1 (Carpet backing cloth (Jute & Synthetic) and Mosquito nets.)	5	3.8095	.16496	0.488	0.744
Category 2 (Blinds and Furniture fabrics)	10	3.5918	.39922		
Category 3 (Fiberfil, pillow components and Stuff toys.)	6	3.8095	.16496		
Category 4 (Mattress and Nonwoven wipes)	6	3.5714	.49487		
Category 5 (HVAC filters Filter cloth for vacuum cleaners.)	9	3.7143	.18070		
Total	**36**	**3.6818**	**.30202**		

The result of the test shows the mean value obtained on Barrier to new entrants across the Product Category manufactured by the Hometech manufacturers.

The statistics shows that the manufacturers of floor coverings and toys and fillings obtained the highest mean value on the barriers to new entrants across the types of speciality products. However, those units manufacturing the, bedding fabrics stand at the minimum mean value.

The results of ANOVA shows F= .488 and Sig. = .744, which is more than .05 (95% level of significance). This indicates that there exists no significant difference in the value of Barrier to new entrants across the Product Category.

Therefore hypothesis H_{01} stands accepted and the alternative hypothesis H_{01a} is rejected. There is no significant difference in the value of barriers to new entrants across the types of Product Category.

H_{06}: There is no significant difference in the value of Barrier to new entrants across the number of years in Hometech industry.

Table 4.7: Barrier to New Entrants Across the Number of Years

No. of Years	N	Mean	Std. Deviation	F	Sig.
0-5 yrs.	4	3.8571	.20203	0.334	0.801
5-10 yrs.	6	3.6190	.29738		
10-15 yrs.	8	3.6190	.42056		
>15 yrs.	18	3.7013	.26691		
Total	**36**	**3.6818**	**.30202**		

The result of the test shows the mean value obtained on barrier to new entrants across the number of years of business by the Hometech manufacturers.

The statistics show that the manufacturers in this industry for less than 5 years obtained the highest mean value on barriers to new entrants. However, those units manufacturing for 5 to 10 and 10 to 15 years stand at the minimum mean value of the barriers to new entry.

The results of ANOVA shows F = .334 and Sig. = .801, which is more than .05 (95% level of significance). This indicates that there is no significant difference in the value of Barrier to new entrants across the number of years in the industry.

Therefore hypothesis H_{01} stands accepted and the alternative hypothesis H_{01a} is rejected. There is no significant difference in the value of Barrier to new entrants across the number of years.

(d) ***Barrier to substitutes with reference to Product Category and number of years.***

H_{07}: There is no significant difference in the value of Barrier to substitutes across the types of Product Category in Hometech industry.

The result of the test shows the mean value obtained on bargaining power of the suppliers across the speciality material manufactured by the Hometech manufacturers.

The statistics shows that the manufacturers of toys and fillings obtained the highest mean value on barriers to substitutes. However, those units manufacturing bedding fabrics stand at the minimum mean value of the bargaining power.

Table 4.8: Barrier to Substitutes with Product Category

Product Category	N	Mean	Std. Deviation	F	Sig.
Category 1 (Carpet backing cloth (Jute & Synthetic) and Mosquito nets.)	6	4.0000	.50000	2.616	0.072
Category 2 (Blinds and Furniture fabrics)	10	3.8571	.37796		
Category 3 (Fiberfil, pillow components and Stuff toys.)	5	4.3333	.57735		
Category 4 (Mattress and Nonwoven wipes)	5	3.1667	.57735		
Category 5 (HVAC filters Filter cloth for vacuum cleaners.)	10	3.8333	.40825		
Total	**36**	**3.8409**	**.52068**		

The results of ANOVA shows F= 2.616 and Sig. = .072, which is more than .05 (95% level of significance). This indicates that there exists no significant difference in the value of Barrier to substitutes across the Product Category.

Therefore hypothesis H_{01} stands accepted and the alternative hypothesis H_{01a} is rejected. There is no significant difference in the value of Barrier to substitutes across the types of Product Category.

H_{08}: There is no significant difference in the value of Barrier to substitutes across the number of years in Hometech industry.

Table 4.9: Barrier to Substitutes Across the Number of Years

No. of Years	N	Mean	Std. Deviation	F	Sig.
0-5 yrs.	4	3.7500	.35355	0.024	0.995
5-10 yrs.	6	3.8333	.57735		
10-15 yrs.	8	3.8333	.25820		
>15 yrs.	18	3.8636	.67420		
Total	**36**	**3.8409**	**.52068**		

The result of the test shows the mean value obtained on bargaining power of the suppliers across the number of years of business by the Hometech manufacturers.

The statistics shows that the manufacturers in this industry since more than 15 years obtained the highest mean value on barriers to substitutes. However, those units manufacturing for less than 5 years stand at the minimum mean value of the barriers to substitutes. We can also observe that on an average there is very little difference between the mean values across the number of years.

The results of ANOVA shows F= .024 and Sig. = .995 which is more than .05 (95% level of significance). This indicates that there is no significant influence of the number of years in the industry on the Barrier to substitutes.

Therefore hypothesis H_{01} stands accepted and the alternative hypothesis H_{01a} is rejected. There is no significant difference in the value of Barrier to substitutes across the number of years.

(e) ***Barrier to competitors with reference to Product Category and number of years.***

H_{09}: There is no significant difference in the value of Barrier to competitors across the types of Product Category in Hometech industry.

Table 4.10: Barrier to Competitors with Product Category

Product Category	N	Mean	Std. Deviation	F	Sig.
Category 1 (Carpet backing cloth (Jute & Synthetic) and Mosquito nets.)	6	3.5556	.19245	1.101	0.388
Category 2 (Blinds and Furniture fabrics)	10	3.6190	.12599		
Category 3 (Fiberfil, pillow components and Stuff toys.)	6	3.6667	.00000		
Category 4 (Mattress and Nonwoven wipes)	6	3.5556	.19245		
Category 5 (HVAC filters Filter cloth for vacuum cleaners.)	8	3.7778	.27217		
Total	**36**	**3.6515**	**.19182**		

The result of the test shows the mean value obtained on bargaining power of the suppliers across the product category manufactured by the Hometech manufacturers.

The statistics shows that the manufacturers of HVAC filter & Filter cloth for vacuum cleaners obtained the highest mean value on barrier to competitors. However, those units manufacturing the category 1 and category 4 products stand at the minimum mean value on barrier to competitors.

The results of ANOVA shows F= 1.101 and Sig. = .388, which is less than .05 (95% level of significance). This indicates that there is a significant influence of the Product Category on the barrier to competitors.

Therefore hypothesis H_{01} stands rejected and the alternative hypothesis H_{01a} is accepted. There is significant difference in the value of Barrier to competitors across the types of Product Category.

H_{10}: There is no significant difference in the value of Barrier to competitors across the number of years in Hometech industry.

Table 4.11: Barrier to Competitors Across the Number of Years

No. of Years	N	Mean	Std. Deviation	F	Sig.
0-5 yrs.	4	3.5000	.23570	0.42	0.741
5-10 yrs.	6	3.6667	.00000		
10-15 yrs.	8	3.6667	.00000		
>15 yrs.	18	3.6667	.25820		
Total	**36**	**3.6515**	**.19182**		

The result of the test shows the mean value obtained on bargaining power of the suppliers across the number of years of business by the Hometech manufacturers.

The statistics shows that the manufacturers in this industry since more than 05 years obtained the highest mean value on barriers to competitors. However, those units manufacturing for less than 5 years stand at the minimum mean value on barriers to competitors.

The results of ANOVA shows F= .42 and Sig. = .741, which is more than .05 (95% level of significance). This indicates that there is no significant influence of the number of years in the industry on the Barrier to competitors.

Therefore hypothesis H_{01} stands accepted and the alternative hypothesis H_{01a} is rejected. There is no significant difference in the value of Barrier to competitors across the number of years.

SUMMARY OF THE HYPOTHESES TESTING

Table 4.12: Summary of Results of Hypothesis Testing

No.	Hypotheses	Results
H_{01}	There is no significant difference in the value of bargaining power of suppliers across the Product Category in Hometech industry.	Accepted
H_{02}	There is no significant difference in the value of bargaining power of suppliers across the number of years in Hometech industry.	Rejected
H_{03}	There is no significant difference in the value of bargaining power of buyers across the Product Category in Hometech industry.	Rejected
H_{04}	There is no significant difference in the value of bargaining power of buyers across the number of years in Hometech industry.	Rejected
H_{05}	There is no significant difference in the value of barriers to new entrants across the Product Category in Hometech industry.	Rejected
H_{06}	There is no significant difference in the value of Barrier to new entrants across the number of years in Hometech industry.	Rejected
H_{07}	There is no significant difference in the value of Barrier to substitutes across the Product Category in Hometech industry.	Rejected
H_{08}	There is no significant difference in the value of Barrier to substitutes across the number of years in Hometech industry.	Rejected
H_{09}	There is no significant difference in the value of Barrier to competitors across the Product Category in Hometech industry.	Accepted
H_{10}	There is no significant difference in the value of Barrier to competitors across the number of years in Hometech industry.	Rejected

CONCLUSION

The foregoing research examined the competitiveness of the Hometech industry in India. Out of the ten hypotheses framed, the first and the ninth are accepted and others are rejected. After statistically examining the hypotheses, inferences are drawn and interpreted in the next chapter which further extends to give suggestion and recommendations for strengthening of the industry.

CHAPTER 5

Interpretation, Problems and Recommendations

INTRODUCTION

After applying the Porter's Five Forces Model on Indian Hometech Industry and statistically analysing the data collected through questionnaire, it becomes necessary to interpret the complete analysis. The interpretation done and conclusions drawn are based on quantitative as well as qualitative data. Quantitative data is statically analysed and the interpretation is based on that. At the time of filling of questionnaire few respondents were hesitant to disclose the facts. The discussions with them added qualitatively to the researcher's data bank. Thus following are the interpretations and conclusions drawn for the total research project conducted.

INTERPRETATION OF THE HYPOTHESIS TESTING AND CONCLUSIONS DRAWN

The environment in which an industry competes is very broad including social as well as economic forces. The macro environment plays relatively stronger role in comparison to the micro environment as external forces usually affect all firms in the industry. The key is found in the differing abilities of firms to deal with them. The state of competition in an industry depends on five basic competitive forces. The collective strength of these forces determine the ultimate profit potential in the industry, where it is measured in terms of long run return on invested capital (Michel E. Porter, 2004).

In the above analysis these forces have been used as hypothesis of the study to measure competitiveness of Hometech industry. The statistical analyses discussed above have been interpreted below:

I. Bargaining power of the suppliers with reference to Product Category and number of years:

A. Across the product category in Hometech industry

The result of the analysis shows that the manufacturers of blinds and furniture fabrics are exposed to strong bargaining powers of the suppliers. This is due to various reasons such as:

(a) The raw material taken from the supplier is expensive and not easily available (most of the spare parts is imported);

(b) Suppliers are few in numbers and is more concentrated than the firms it sells to; (Suppliers selling to more fragmented buyers will usually be able to exert considerable influence in prices, quality and terms)

(c) There exists situation that the options in terms of suppliers is restricted to manufacturers;

(d) The raw material has to be imported from other nations. Various blind manufacturers are only fabricators and do not manufacture fabric. Various components used in a blind such as hangers, spacers, head rails, interlocking chain, sliding channel, runner, end cap set, bottom weight, tilting chain, etc. are though domestically procured but heavily imported from Taiwan, China and few European countries. Synthetic coated fabrics strips are imported from Taiwan and China. Ready blinds are also imported from Germany, Australia and USA. All the players in the organised segment import over 95% of their sales.

(e) In case of furniture fabrics over 90% of artificial leather and around 82% of flock fabric are imported from China. Taiwan has a share of about 5% in the imports of artificial leather followed by Korea, Canada and USA. USA and

Belgium are also major suppliers of flock fabric. Over 85% of the velvet fabric is imported from China. Significant imports also take from Italy, Hong Kong and Turkey.

(f) The spare parts or raw material provided by suppliers form an important input to the buyers for manufacturing process or product quality.

(g) We always consider the suppliers as other firms, but labour must be recognised as a supplier as well, and one that exerts great power in many industries (Michel E. Porter, 2004). For the manufacture of blinds and furniture fabrics firms need well trained and technically sound labour. There is scarcity of highly skilled employees in this industry in India. This gives them a better bargaining power over the producers.

These are the reasons why suppliers are in commanding position and try to control or bargain the terms and conditions for the supply of raw material to the firms.

In contrast to this the suppliers to the units producing Fiberfil, pillow components and Stuff toysare less strong in terms of bargaining power. The reasons are the large quantity of suppliers, easy availability of raw material, easy production of raw material, whichis usually available in the local market. The labour required for this segment is not highly skilled. Little training is given to make them good enough for work.

Statistical test also give us an idea that the bargaining power of the suppliers is significantly influenced by the nature of raw material supplied or the type of products manufactured. This can be concluded on the basis that responses vary across the product category of the Hometech industry. It is found that raw material or the inputs that have to be majorly imported from other countries or whose production needs highly skilled employees face stronger negotiations from suppliers and the situation is reverse if inputs and labour is available sufficiently.

B. Across the number of years in Hometech industry

From the results of the analysis we may conclude that those units which have been manufacturing the Hometech products for 5 or less than 5 years are exposed to stronger bargaining powers of the suppliers in comparison to those manufacturers who are in the industry for more than 5 years. The suppliers of the raw material/ inputs have the least bargaining power with the manufacturers who are for more than 15 years in the industry. Thus reflecting that the number of years in the industry play an important role in deciding the bargaining power of the suppliers to the manufacturers. The older a firm in the industry the better it can negotiate with the suppliers. The firms with lesser number of years in the industry may be due to lack of experience or weaker negotiating skills have to give in to the terms and conditions of the suppliers. Though there is difference in the bargaining power of the suppliers across the number of years, the mean variation is not significant.

Further the statistical results also reflect that bargaining powers of the suppliers is not significantly influenced by the number of years in the industry. This can be concluded on the basis that responses do not vary much across the number of years of the Hometech industry.

Thus old or new firms in the Hometech industry face strong bargaining power of the suppliers/labours due to above discussed reasons. Strongest of all is that there is heavy dependency on other countries for technology, raw material and skilled or well equipped workers. This is the biggest limitations of the industry.

II. Bargaining power of the buyers with reference to Product Category and number of years

A. Across the product category in Hometech industry

From the statistical results conclusion may be drawn that the producers of Fiberfil, pillow components and Stuff toys are exposed to strong bargaining powers of the buyers. The reasons are that the buyers' concentration is stronger than the firms'; there is limited number of buyers with huge volumes of purchases; close substitute products are easily available; there are large numbers of sellers of these products. Fiberfil has low penetration in the Indian industry.However, with increasing awareness about the product benefits its penetration is expected to increase in future. Thus, the domestic market size of Fiberfil is estimated to be 140,300 MT in 2012-13 (growing at 5 - 6% year on year). The market potential in 2012-13 is at Rs. 840 crore. This segment exports little quantity.

Based on interaction with the industry experts and key industry players the domestic market size for stuffed toys is estimated at Rs. 420 crore or 60 million pieces. On account of rising disposable income and increasing preference for stuffed toys amongst both youngsters and kids the stuff toy manufacturers have been witnessing double digit growth rates in the recent years and the industry is growing at a CAGR of 15%.

In comparison the buyers of Hometech producers for Blinds, Furniture fabrics, Mattress, Nonwoven wipes, HVAC filters and Filter cloth for vacuum cleaners have less strong bargaining powers.

In contrast to this the buyers of Hometech material for Carpet backing cloth (Jute & Synthetic) and Mosquito nets have least bargaining power. This is because of the reasons that they are least concentrated, large in numbers with small quantity purchases or lesser number of sellers. The growth in the carpet industry is the key demand driver for CBC. The Indian carpet industry is mainly driven by exports. Around 95% of the carpets made in India are exported majorly to USA. The carpet export witnessed a decline in recent years because of rupee appreciation against dollar.

We can see that the there is a little difference in the mean values between the bargaining powers of the buyers across the different product categories of the Hometech industry. Further, statistical test also give us an idea that the bargaining power of the buyers is not significantly influenced by the type of product category in the industry. Across the product category it is observed that bargaining power is high if there is:

(a) Concentration or large volume purchases by buyers;

(b) The product it purchases from the industry represent a significant fraction of the buyers costs or purchases;

(c) The product it purchases from the industry is standard or undifferentiated and they are sure that they can always find alternative suppliers, may play one company against another;

(d) The industry's product is unimportant to the quality of the buyers' products or services;

(e) The buyers are well informed about the market.

B. Across the number of years in Hometech industry

The bargaining power of the buyers strengthens with passage of years. The larger the number of years in the industry the strongly it can bargain or negotiate its terms and conditions. The statistical result exhibits that the firms that are for more than 15 years in the industry have comparatively strong bargaining power than those with less than 5 years of entry.

Further the statistical results exhibit that though there is a difference in the bargaining powers of the buyers with the number of years but it is not significant. Thus we may conclude that the number of years in the industry do not significantly influence the bargaining power of the buyers on the firms.

III. Barrier to new entrants with reference to Product Category and number of years:

A. Across the product category in Hometech industry

New entrants to an industry bring new capacity, the desire to gain market share, and often substantial resources. Prices can be bid down or incumbents' costs inflated as a result, reducing profitability. The threat of entry into an industry depends on the barriers to entry that are present, coupled with the reaction from existing competitors that can the entrant may expect. Factors that can limit the threat of new entrants are known as barriers to entry.

The statistical results reflect that firms producing floor coverings, stuff toys and filling material pose strongest barrier to new entrants across the various types of speciality materials. Rest have a comparatively less strong barrier to entry but the variation is not too large. The reasons responsible for this are:

(a) There is lesser access to necessary inputs and technology; technology to produce has to be imported from other countries;

(b) Huge capital (investment) is required to set up the plant;

(c) Economies of scale play an important role in every function of a business, including manufacturing, purchasing, research and distribution. The new entrants fear to enter at a large scale and risk strong reaction from existing firms. If it comes in at a small scale then it has to suffer cost disadvantage. There exist established firms with brand identification and customer loyalty which leads to product differentiation. This creates a barrier to entry by forcing entrants to spend heavily to overcome existing customers' loyalties.

For example Reliance Industries Limited is the largest manufacturer of Virgin PSF Fiberfil in India. The company markets its product under the brand name Recron. Some other major manufacturers engaged in manufacture of virgin PSF and regenerated PSF are Ganesh Polytex, Arora Fibres limited, Alliance Fibres, Nirmal fibres Private limited. They pose strong barriers to new entrants. Major producers of Carpet backing cloth are Ludlow Jute, Birla Corporation and Gloster Jute. They pose great threat to new entrants.

(d) In some product category like floor coverings, stuff toys and filling material pose strongest barrier to new entrants. Evan the imports or entrants from the other countries are discouraged on the grounds that the established players have favourable access to raw material, proprietary product technology, favourable locations, government subsidies, etc.

The results also indicate that the different Hometech product category have no/little significant influence on the barrier to new entrants in the industry. It may be concluded that all sectors of the industry impose almost equal barrier on the new entrants.

B. Across the number of years in Hometech industry

On the basis of the statistical results it may be drawn that numbers of years hardly influence the entry of new entrepreneurs or producers in the industry. Those within five years in the industry pose stronger barriers in comparison to those who are for longer period in the industry. This is because of the proprietary learning curve. Since this industry is still in nascent stage and technical in nature, the proprietor's need to be adequately trained and well equipped with the production techniques. Few or many years, new producers always remain cautious before investing in this industry.

Further the statistical results also reflect that numbers of years in the industry have no significant influence on imposing threat or barrier to new entrants.This can be concluded on the basis that responses do not vary across the number of years of the Hometech industry.

IV. Barrier to substitutes with reference to Product Category and number of years:

A. Across the product category in Hometech industry

All firms in an industry are competing with industries producing substitute products. Substitutes limit the potential returns of an industry by placing the ceiling on the prices firms in the industry can profitably charge.(Michel E. Porter, 2004). Substitutes not only limit profits in normal times, but they also reduce the bonanza an industry can reap in boom times.

The result of the analysis shows that the manufacturers of Fiberfil, pillow components and stuff toys impose strongest barrier to substitutes. Whereas, the producers of mattress and nonwoven wipes impose minimum barrier to substitutes. The reasons are the relative value /price of a substitute compared to the speciality material of different segments of the industry, the cost of switching to the substitutes and the buyers propensity to switch.

Further the results also prove that though there is difference to the level of barriers across the various product categories but there is no significant influence of these product categories on the barriers to substitutes.

B. Across the number of years in Hometech industry

Whether the firm in the industry is for less than five years or more than fifteen years, barriers to substitutes continue to be almost same. We may conclude that it hardly affect whether the firm has remained for longer or shorter time period in the industry. The results of the analysis shows that the firm's being for the number of years in the Hometech industry pose no significant influence on the barriers to substitutes.

V. Barrier to competitors with reference to Product Category and number of years:

A. Across the product category in Hometech industry

Rivalry occurs because one or more competitors either feels the pressure or sees the opportunity to improve position. In most industries, competitive moves by one firm have noticeable effects on its competitors and thus may incite retaliation or efforts to counter the move.

The analytical results prove that there is intense rivalry between different product segments in the industry. Out of all product categories manufacturers of HVAC filter& Filter cloth for vacuum cleanershave most intense rivalry whereas those units manufacturing the Carpet backing cloth (Jute & Synthetic), Mosquito nets, Mattress and Nonwoven wipes stand at the minimum mean value on barrier to competitors i.e. least rivalry existing.

Intense rivalry is the result of a number interacting structural factors. Some of them existing in the Hometech industry are:

(a) The filter media is imported from Germany, Netherlands, Taiwan, China and USA. The imports from Netherlands account for around 40% of the imports. The HEPA filters are imported from Malaysia, China, USA, and Netherlands. Similarly Filter fabrics used in vacuum cleaners are not manufactured by vacuum cleaner manufacturers and are outsourced. The filter fabrics are majorly imported. The exports from India of HVAC filters and filter media are negligible. (Final Report on Baseline

Survey of the Technical Textile industry in India (2009), March, Office of the Textile Commissioner

From the qualitative information it was found out that the input for HVAC filters, filter media, vacuum cleaner, etc., are majorly imported from other countries. India is seen as a big market with bright prospects for further demand by the sellers or importing countries. In order to keep a tight control on Indian market there is intense rivalry amongst them. The foreign competitors who export in to the industry play an important role in industry competition.

(b) Whatever is produced in the country is done by few manufacturers who are equally balanced competitors leading to intense competition.

(c) Technical textiles industry is facing a slow industry growth in India. Hometech industry has grown in the past years but not significantly. There are only around 60 manufacturers in this industry. This turns competition in to a market share game for firms seeking expansion. Market share competition is highly volatile.

(d) HVAC filters, filter media, vacuum cleaner, etc., is perceived as a commodity or near commodity, choice by the buyer is largely based on price and services and this creates intense price and service competition whereas in the products like Carpet backing cloth (Jute & Synthetic), Mosquito nets, Mattress and Nonwoven wipes, which have product differentiation, on the other hand, creates lesser competitive warfare because buyers have preferences and loyalties to particular sellers.

(e) Rivalry in an industry becomes even more volatile if the number of firms have high stake in achieving success there.

(f) Hometech industry has high exit barriers because of its specialised assets. Assets highly specialised usually have low liquidation values or high cost of transfer or conversion. It is observed that when exit barriers are high, excess capacity does not leave the industry, and companies that loose the competitive battle do not give up. Instead they hang on.

Further the results also prove that the barrier to competitors or rivalry is significantly influenced by the different product category.This can be concluded on the basis that responses vary across the product category of the Hometech industry.

C. Across the number of years in Hometech industry

The results of the analysis prove that the number of years in the industry does not significantly influence the firm's barrier to the competitors. Whether the firm remains in the industry for less than five or more than fifteen years, the barriers remain same. Further, the results of the analysis shows that the firm's being for the number of years in the Hometech industry pose no significant influence on the barriers to competitors or rivalry.

MAJOR PROBLEMS FACED BY THE HOMETECH INDUSTRY IN INDIA

On survey while interviewing the producers, sellers and exporters of the Hometech products the researcher found that some root problems are existing in the industry which are responsible for the slow growth rate of the industry in India. Some of them are discussed below:

1. Multi fiber agreement (MFA)

The quotas were fixed by developed countries, which curtailed growth of exports from Reliance during 2002-03 and 2003-04. Reliance as an integrated producer of polyester was strong enough to strengthen its position as the second largest producer of the polyester (fiber and yarn) and was able to take advantage from the opportunities that lie ahead. (Reliance Industries ltd, 2003).The much-awaited abolition of the textile quota by the US, the EU and Canada was applied from January2005, which provided big opportunity for the industry to have access to global textile market.

2. Lack of awareness

The primary reason for low consumption of Hometech Textiles in India is lack of awareness about the application of Hometech textiles and its benefits for the end product and user. Although, the Textile Commissioners Office under the Ministry of Textiles, Government of India is trying its best to create awareness about technical textiles by conducting training workshops, seminars and conferences, but it is not positively increasing the awareness about Hometech segment. Information on domestic and foreign market demand for various Hometech textiles products is not available to the investors. While the textile commissioner's office has recently published a baseline survey report on technical textiles of the domestic market but it is not sufficient to attract Indian investors towards Hometech textiles when the investment costs on European machines are very high. Hence, international market survey reports covering international market supply and demand information must be made available to the Indian Investors to create a production and market base of Hometech Textiles in India.(Marimuthu, 2010)

3. Lack of demand

There is lack of demand for Home tech textiles as it is only used as an alternative when traditional home textiles are not appropriate. This is mainly because of lack of awareness among the consumers about the benefits of using Hometech textiles. This lack of awareness is hindering the potential demand of Hometech textiles in India. Due to lack of clear cut policy on specifications and standardization of Hometech textiles, the quality benchmark for Home tech textiles technology are not available. The investors have thus no clear-cut idea about the potential growth in the sector. The promotion of Hometech textiles is essential for not only Technical textile growth, economic growth, employment generation and increasing exports but in the larger public interest for home furnishing, trendy decoration, public safety, security, hygiene and comfort. Thus, there is great need for providing proper regulatory framework to safeguard the interests of consumers. (National Council of Applied Economic Research, 2009)

4. Higher cost of raw material

The conventional home textiles are export intensive, on the contraryHometech textiles are import intensive products.

Many products required as raw material for this industry are imported from the foreign countries (i.e., knitted fabric, fur fabric, filter fabric for vacuum cleaner, woven fabric etc.).The major production of this industry is providing to the domestic demand. However, the large-scale units are engaged in producing various Hometech products like fibrefill, stuffed toys, non-woven wipes, floor coverings etc. but still many of the Hometech textiles products that are not produced domestically in adequate quantity have to be imported to accomplish the domestic demand. This makes raw materials for Hometech textiles costly in India, which is one of the main reasons for low consumption of Hometech textiles. Hence, there is sharp need for easy availability of specialized raw materials for Hometech textiles in the domestic market. For this, adequate fiscal measures should be taken to promote this sector. (National Council of Applied Economic Research, 2009)

5. Lack of Research and Development

A major concern related to development of Hometech products is lack of indigenous research and development in the area of Hometech textiles. Further, the technology required for manufacturing of most of the Hometech textiles is proprietary and very expensive. High cost and low demand have also discouraged Indian players to produce Hometech textiles indigenously. (National Council of Applied Economic Research, 2009)

6. Lack of skilled labour or manpower

The manpower available in India is not too skilled in their technical and managerial skill which is one of the major hurdles for the expansion of Hometech sector in India. As this is a high-tech segment and very skilled workforce is required for manufacturing Hometech products. India having a large population because of which labour that cheaper but these people are needed to be trained and educated to conform to the specifications, the quality control and quality culture of the Hometech textiles. It is noticed that the Hometech textiles products with high production levels in India with considerable exports are usually commodity products that are not very Research and Development intensive. These products include stuffed toys, jute carpet backing, synthetic carpet backing, blinds etc. Hence, value addition in our Hometech textiles product is relatively much low as compared to our competitors. To get progress in Hometech segment there is need for preparing a strong pool of skilled labor which is suitable for the development of a highly innovative and Research and Development intensive domestic Hometech textiles industry. (National Council of Applied Economic Research, 2009)

7. Lack of regulatory norms by the Government

One of the reasons for low penetration of Hometech textiles is lack of regulatory norms by the government to boost the market development of Hometech in India. For example, there are no regulations in place for fire safety of Furniture and Furnishings. There are also no regulations for the use of furniture intended for private use in a dwelling, including children's furniture, beds, head-boards of beds, mattresses (of any size), sofa-beds, futons and other convertibles, nursery furniture, garden furniture which is suitable for use in a dwelling etc. which do not mandate the use of Hometech textile products but encourages the use of these products as home tech products are produced to meet these standards. There are also no set Flammability Test Procedure for Seating Furniture for Use in Public Occupancies etc. which mandate the use of Hometech products meeting the set standards, resistance requirements etc.(Office of the Textile Commissioner, 2009).

8. Lack of Processes, machineries and equipment

Production of Hometech textiles needs conventional as well as state-of-the-art equipment depending on the application, desirable quality parameters, fulfilment of functional parameters, when one considers that Hometech textiles cover common applications like floor coverings, jute carpet backings etc. to complex applications like fire retardant furniture seating, synthetic carpet backings, filter fabrics etc. For the production of Hometech textiles, degree of accuracy required for the end use requirement and rigidity of the leading specifications, the product processes, machinery and equipment are to be selected. However, it is observed that for large areas of home textiles application, India has a quite good infrastructure of spinning, weaving, knitting, wet-processing, impregnation and lamination etc. but it is not adequate for producing the varieties of Hometech Textiles. Existing raw materials, machinery and know-how are needed to be geared to produce certain range of Hometech textiles in India and to ensure adequate impact in globalization. (Ministry of Textiles, 1999)

9. Lack of Technology and Know-how

The share of unorganised sector in production of the Hometech textiles in the country is around 40per cent in which scale of operation is limited and technology is relatively outdated. The major obstacle for expansion of the sector is low demand, which clarifies the high share of operations in small-scale sector in order to meet the skinny demand spread all over the country. This is also the cause for huge technological gap between technology used in competitor countries and that used in India.There is great need of massive technology up gradation in the sector and government should play a major role in it by providing technology/consultancy support to manufacturers for development of Hometech textiles. Moreover, there is vast requirement to encourage modernization in this sector by providing priority or additional incentives for Hometech under Technology Up gradation Fund Scheme (TUFS). (Ministry of Textiles, 1999)

10. Lack of Testing facilities

One important feature in both development activities and production of Hometech textiles is devotion to certain specified standards for dependable and sustained performance of such products for intended purpose. The international standards for most of the common products have been laid down by agencies like ASTM, BS, EN, Deutsche Industries norm (DIN), GHOST etc. (Ministry of Textiles, 1999).Because of wide varieties of products using technical textiles, the centralized test laboratories are not paying attention towards Hometech segment to cater all such testing services and performance evaluation. It is, therefore, vigilant on the part of the producers of Hometech textiles to set up the essential testing rigs and equipment to keep a strict control over the quality. As far as India is concerned, small and medium scale units are not able to afford very expensive cost of such equipment, centralized test facilities which are required to be created in strategic locations.

11. Lack of Quality assurance

The products of Hometech textiles are ruled by much stricter tolerance of parameters and will, therefore, have little value, if they do not match to the rigid specifications. Therefore, it must be ensured that the quality assurance system incorporated by the manufacturers of Hometech textiles is grounded on quality management based on zero-defect concept. Unfortunately, Indian Hometech manufacturers, particularly medium and small scale are not able to afford the in-built quality assurance system for producing Hometech products because of the very high cost. (Ministry of Textiles, 1999)

12. Bottlenecks for Entrepreneurs

In order to promote the production of Hometech textiles, the primary need would be to catch the attention of entrepreneurs in the field of Hometech textiles. Entrepreneurs are still keeping away from the Hometech textiles in view of the following hindrances (Rakshit, Hira, and Gangopadhyay, 2007):

(a) The aspects of Hometech textile and marketing are highly multifaceted and Indian entrepreneurs in textiles have not exposed with this difficult situation therefore, they have genuine doubts and anxieties about success in such ventures;

(b) Hometech textiles demand specific raw materials, machinery and equipment, which are mostly imported and therefore, requiring huge capital towards the project cost;

(c) Hometech textiles being at a growing stage in India, innovation of technology for product development and establishing specific markets with enough volumes require huge working capital for a minimum period of 5 years, so the entrepreneur could anticipate fruits of high value addition usually associated with Hometech textiles. Moreover, market development will require continuous promotional efforts, which need considerable investments as well as lead time;

(d) The developed countries have achieved a saturation point in mass of the Hometech textiles and they are moving towards developing countries including India in a competitive manner in globalized markets. They are well-experienced in various aspects of Hometech textiles and financial strength, while Indian entrepreneurs have little or no experience or knowledge in this direction;

(e) The existing norms and mandatory requirements of Hometech textiles in India are either outdated or non-existing that makes difficult task for entrepreneurs of launching home tech textiles to end users in the Indian market.(Rakshit, Hira, and Gangopadhyay, 2007)

13. Absence of Centres of Excellence for Home tech Textiles

The field of Technical Textiles is so vast that, unlike conventional textile materials, it would not be possible to provide support services for all fields from one organisation. Therefore, it would be appropriate that numbers of centres should be opened across the country to integrate overall development of the field (Rakshit, Hira and Gangopadhyay, 2007). Though, there are number of IITS/Textiles Institutes and eight Centers of Excellences (COEs) present in India i.e. Geotech (BTRA), Agrotech (SASMIRA), Meditech (SITRA) &Protech (NITRA), Composite (ATIRA), Non-Woven (DKTE), Indutech (PSG College) and Sportech which are providing latest testing facilities national/international accreditation, information centre, facilities for training, prototype development facilities etc. but unfortunately, there is no single centre of excellence for Hometech Textiles in India.

14. Quota regime for exports of textile/clothing

The quota regimes for exports of textile/clothing (Multi fiber agreement) adversely affected the performance of the companies during the years 2002-03 and 2003-04 by restricting exports and its abolition by 2005 provided big opportunity for the company to expand its growth both in exports and domestic market (Ginni filaments ltd, 2004).Since 2006, the raw material i.e. manmade fiber, cotton and viscose the was easy available for the company due to the abolition of quantitative restrictions under MFA and the positive fiscal changes made by the Government which allowed company moving towards consolidation, expansion and restructuring (Ginni filaments ltd, 2006).

15. Fluctuations in cotton/cotton yarn prices

Cotton as an agricultural product and raw material for the company, witnessed fall in production during 2002-03 causing spurt in prices due to the adverse weather conditions. The performance of the company during the year 2005 under review were affected mainly due to higher cost of cotton procured in the previous cotton season and thereafter steep fall in cotton and cotton yarn prices resulting into huge stock losses.Procurement of cotton during the season is necessitated to ensure consistency in the quality of yarn demanded by the valued overseas customers. Despite the higher world production of cotton during the crop year 2004-05, the yarn prices of the companies witnessed a significant downward trend (Ginni filaments ltd, 2005).Though, the industry was in critical position during the year 2008 due to the unprecedented increase in cotton but in 2011–12 there were wild fluctuation in prices of cotton and cotton yarn.Hence, the year under review was not healthy for cotton yarn business during first three quarters. The fluctuation in the prices of raw cotton due to global scenario and government's policies regarding export regulations of cotton and cotton yarn were remain a major threat area for textile industry. The company procured cotton during peck cotton season to maintain the quality of cotton yarn as company is predominantly export oriented.However, the subsequent steep fall in cotton and cotton yarn prices resulted into substantial stock losses(Ginni filaments ltd, 2012).

16. Increase in fuel prices

Although, the companies achieved better performance despite steep increase in fuel prices during the years 2006 and 2007 but they resulted into increase in cost of power generation in the captive power plant of the company, which partially affected the margin of textile units with captive power generation(Ginni filaments ltd, 2006).Therefore, the industry was in critical position during 2007-08 due to the extraordinary increase in fuel prices.

17. Depreciation of US dollar

The industry was hardly hit by the rapid and sharp appreciation of Indian rupee against US dollar and the increase in interest rates from the beginning of 2007 because it is highly export oriented industry which eroded its cost competitiveness (Ginni filaments ltd, 2008).

18. Global recession

During the year 2008-09, the global economic slowdown and the lack of demand in the domestic economy affected the company's performance adversely. However, because of timely action of the government and increase in demand from both export and domestic markets the situation started improving in the next year i.e. 2009-10 which resulted in escalation of prices in recent months and helped in retrieving some lost ground. But, export of the company got down during this year due to the demand contraction in the global markets (Ginni filaments ltd, 2010). Because of global recession in the years 2007-08 and 2008-09 the inventory level of the company reduced substantially but demand started improving during the year 2011.

19. Unhealthy competition from unorganised sector

Most of the small scale units still use natural materials such as coir, sisal, wool, cotton, kapok, glass and horsehair as filling materials for upholstered furniture and other applications which create unhealthy competition resulting reduce demand and profit of other firms.The manufacturing units of the company, which are engaged in producing needle punch wall-to-wall carpets, are mostly located in unorganised sector that causes quality compromises while offering attractive prices by the company. This has damaged customer confidence in nonwoven needle punch carpets. The company's philosophy is to attain high level of customer satisfaction therefore; they have had to cut prices for meeting competition and maintaining quality product to the consumer. The company is importing loop pile carpets to meet customer desires in this product category and to enhance the declining revenue per unit of sale, which also offers higher value addition to the company (Uniproducts India ltd, 2003).

20. Entry of new units

Several manufacturing units have come up in recent times in various specified areas enjoying exemption from Excise Duty, Sales Tax, Concessional Power Tariff, Capital Subsidy etc. offering the fiber at low prices, promoting the threat of new entrants.(Arora fibres ltd, 2007).

21. Absence of Research and Development

There is no activity on Research and development, which is a major reason of low demand and production of the polyester staple fiber for the company.

22. Low value imports from other Asian and South East Asian countries

However, the company Uniproducts India ltd. is the only indigenous producer of Thermo bond interlinings, but it is facing severe competition from low value imports from other Asian and South East Asian countries. Thus, the company finalized sources for import of certain grades of thermo bond interlinings not being manufactured by them as a measure to supplement the range and to boost the revenues for upholding the dominance in this segment (Uniproducts India Ltd., 2003).

The interlinings and cover stocks are imported at cheaper prices in India, which badly affects the demand of these products manufactured by the company. Therefore, the company is importing interlinings for meeting market demand and supplementing this range produced by them (Uniproducts India ltd, 2004).

23. Tsunami in Japan-2011

During 2011-12, the performance of the company affected adversely because of some unwanted events. The supply chains of Honda Motors and Toyota Motors in India were badly affected due to the tsunami in Japan 2011 and resultantly the vehicle production of these companies was very low in the first quarter. Moreover, some car producers like Hyundai Motors, and specially Maruti, were affected because of labor unrest, which was heavy load for their production and sales. Besides, the production of Honda Motors affected adversely during the year because of floods in Thailand that resulted non-availability of components. As the Uniproducts is a supplier of car carpets to all these car manufactures and that is why sales of the company were impacted during the financial year 2011-12. Furthermore, some of the car that was going to launch in 2011 was postponed for 2012due to this disorder, which further affected the sales of the company. In addition, profitability of the company also declined due to the high interest as a result company maintained its manpower for the predictable capacity and bear the salary cost because these conditions could not be projected(Uniproducts India ltd, 2012).

24. Cheaper imported goods

During 2005, the company Premier poly films ltd. Witnessed low profit due to the stiff competition from indigenous manufacturers and cheap imported goods (Premier polyfilms Ltd., 2005). During 2011, dumping of imported material in the market and detrimental competition from domestic producers due to over capacity were the main factors of low profit margins and sales (Premier polyfilms ltd, 2011). During 2012, the company could not increase price of its products independently because of the domestic and imported products competition (Premier poly films Ltd., 2012).

25. Foreign exchange fluctuations and interest rate risk

The earnings of Reliance industries in all businesses are connected with US dollars. The company purchases crude oil (key input) in US dollars, their export revenues are in foreign currency and even local prices are based on import parity prices, they also have a large portion of the debt in foreign currency for which company takes on liability management transactions and structured derivatives on an ongoing basis (Reliance Industries ltd, 2007). In addition, a majority of the RIL's borrowings is floating rate debt and hence is exposed to upward movement in interest rates (Reliance Industries ltd, 2012). Therefore, changes in the exchange rate between the US Dollar and the Indian rupee and interest rate risk adversely affected Reliance's results of operations and financial condition during the years 2007, 2008, 2009, 2010, 2011 and 2012.

RECOMMENDATIONS AND SUGGESTIONS

After the analysis of current competitive state of the Indian Hometech Industry with five competitive forces, Industry can search for options to influence these forces in their own interest. Although industry-specific business models often limit options, the own strategy can change the impact of competitive forces on the organisation. The objective is to reduce the power of competitive forces in positive direction.The options of an organisation are determined not only by the external market environment, but also by its own internal resources, competences and objectives ("Porter's Five Forces", 2012).

Similarly, the Hometech industry, in order to enhance and strengthen its competence in the Indian as well as International market, needs to influence these five forces of competitiveness. Following are some recommendations and suggestions by the researcher to the industry in this direction (according to five forces):

1. Reducing the Bargaining Power of Suppliers:

(a) It is discovered that in Hometech the suppliers of blinds and furniture fabrics have very strong bargaining power over the buyers. The reasons being that buyers are scattered and few in number. In order to enhance their capital base and production capacity the small firms can move in to partnering with each other. This would make them stronger and more concentrated to negotiate with their suppliers.

(b) The industry is in the nascent stage in India. Most of the raw material for technical products are either imported or purchased from well established, large scale manufacturers. It necessitates to explore and understand the manufacturers or suppliers. The buyers must build knowledge of suppliers' cost structures and their methods (including supply techniques). This would surely help them to prepare strategies and plan orders accordingly. When the suppliers are in the foreign country, it becomes important to understand macro business environment of that country also.

(c) Buyers may also unite and move for 'supply chain management' and 'supply chain training' for better negotiations with their respective suppliers.

(d) The industry needs to strengthen its 'Research and Development' segment. Presently the India Hometech industry is spending huge amount on importing technology if possible. Otherwise it has to import spare parts that cannot be developed here. This heavily adds to the cost of production of the products, especially those which are more technical in nature. Once investment is done in R & D, much outflow of capital can be saved and at the same time dependency on foreign suppliers will be reduced.

(e) Business people and investors must be promoted and encouraged by the government through various promotional schemes e.g. tax holidays/concessions, SEZ, FTZ, etc., to produce the inputs which are imported after paying high prices. If such items are manufactured here, it will significantly help the buyers to reduce their costs.

2. Reducing the Bargaining Power of buyers

This happens only when the buyers' concentration is stronger than the firms'; there is limited number of buyers with huge volumes of purchases; close substitute products are easily available; and there are large numbers of sellers of these products. Some useful measures that can be adopted are:

(a) Partnering may also be used as a tool by sellers to strengthen themselves against concentrated buyers. It may be recommended for both suppliers and Buyers.

(b) In order to negotiate better it also becomes important for sellers to thoroughly understand and follow 'Supply chain management'. This will surely facilitate in grappling more share in the market.

(c) In some of the product categories of Hometech industry brand loyalty plays an important role. The sellers, by providing qualitative services must create and later increase loyalty of their customers. This can be gradually earned by buyers by providing quality assurance in their products, after sales services, discount and festive offers, most reasonable/competitive prices, etc. Once the customers become loyal to the seller, negotiation and rest of the dealings become easy for both the parties.

(d) In addition to the above one may also increase incentives and value added to the products.

(e) Another technique that may be adopted by the sellers to minimise bargaining power of the buyers is to cut down powerful intermediaries (go directly to customer). This would call for greater efforts towards customers, huge capital investment and supply of material in bulk. Once in direct contact with the buyers, things can be handled more profitably with better chunk of the market.

3. Reducing the Treat of New Entrants

It was found that firms producing floor coverings, stuff toys and filling material pose strongest barrier to new entrants across the various types of speciality materials. Rest have a comparatively less strong barrier to entry but the variation is not too large. In order to make these barriers more strong or reduce the threat of new entrants, following recommendations are made:

(a) The small manufacturers will have to expand their production capacity/plant in such a way so as to have minimum efficient scales of operations. Economies of scale play an important role in every function of a business, including manufacturing, purchasing, research and distribution. The new entrants fear to enter at a large scale and risk strong reaction from existing firms. If it comes in at a small scale then it has to suffer cost disadvantage. This shall keep the new entrants away.

(b) Producers will have to create a marketing/brand image. As already discussed above, brand loyalty helps in strengthening goodwill of the business. It attracts the customers to buy from same old seller, discouraging the new seller in the market. Customer's loyalty acts as a barrier to new entrants.

(c) From legal point of view a seller can create barrier by patenting its products.

(d) To discourage the new entrant in the industry, the suppliers of Hometech products may have a strong tie up amongst themselves.The tie up would mean coordination with other suppliers in terms of price, supply, market share, etc. A sort of cartel to discourage a new entrant.

(e) In a similar way there could be a tie up with distributor of the product to reduce the threat of new entrants.

(f) For firms retaliation tactics can always prove beneficial to fight new entrants. Retaliation tactics could be like price cut, incentives, marketing strategies, etc.

4. Reducing the Threat of Substitutes"

Hometech industry has great threat to close substitute because of the nature of the products produce. Some of the measures suggested to minimize this competitive force are:

(a) Appropriate and strong legal actions must be taken by the firms to protect themselves.

(b) Existing firms if required must increase switching costs of the product.

(c) Alliances or partnering can be a wise decision to dissolve the threat of substitutes. Alliances is always better than competing cut throat.

(d) It is necessary for the firms to conduct customer surveys to learn about their taste and preferences. They should design or modify the products according to their preferences so that they do not easily switch to substitutes.

(e) Firms can also penetrate substitute market and influence from within.

(f) In order to discourage the substitute products a firm should accentuate differences (real or perceived) through strong marketing techniques. The difference has to be created in the minds of the customers to create their preferences over their products.

5. Reducing the Competitive Rivalry between Existing Players

(a) Firms in the Indian Hometech industry should avoid price competition amongst themselves. Price war leads to price cut which ultimately reduces the profit margins of the firms.

(b) It becomes important for the firms to differentiate their products from one another to buy out competition. This eases out the rivalry.

(c) Market concentration also aggravates the competition amongst rivals. Instead of focussing on same market segments firms should diversify and focus on different segments. This would surely reduce the competition amongst rivals.

(d) Communication with competitors might also help in reducing competitive pressure. Instead of fighting one may coordinate to make the road smooth.

SUGGESTIONS FOR IMPROVING THE ECONOMIC POSITION OF HOMETECH INDUSTRY IN GENERAL

After making recommendations specific to competitive forces to reduce their impact, now the researcher goes further to recommend for the economic betterment of the Hometech industry in general. This would in return help to make the industry more competitive. Some of them are as follows:

1. In order to get economies of large-scale production, the home tech firms will have to try to increase the production. It will help in reaping the benefit of economies of scale and at the same time raise the rate of return on capital employed.
2. In order to increase the financial effectiveness of the companies, it is suggested to control the cost of goods sold and operating expenses.
3 The managers of the firms must adopt cost reduction techniques in their companies to bring down the prices of the Hometech products and get more competitive.
4. In order to enjoy better operational efficiency of the assets and capital employed, it is always advisable to enlarge the sales quantity. This can be achieved only when producers explore new markets/market segments. US and EU are the major buyers of Indian Hometech Products. But any dip in their demands (may be due to recession, exchange rate, etc.) adversely affects our exporters. New markets have to be explored and penetrated.
5. The power and fuel cost has to be cut down. For this companies will have to find out other alternatives means. In this regards the government of India will have to step down to provide power at subsidised rate and minimise power cut.

6. The selected Hometech companies are suggested to try and match the amount of working capital with the sales trends. For this purpose, where there is a deficit of working capital, they should try to build on adequate amount while, if there is an excessive working capital, it should be invested either in trade securities or should be used to repay borrowings.
7. In order to reduce factory overheads and to utilize their fixed assets properly, it is suggested that the companies should try to utilize their production capacity fully.
8. The burden of interest has produced a worsening effect and reduced the percentage of net profit. It is suggested that the companies should try to increase the owner's fund to reduce the interest burden gradually.
9. To strengthen the financial performance of the companies, long-term funds have to be used to finance core current assets and a part of temporary current assets. The companies should try to reduce the oversized short-term loans and advances and get rid of the risk by arranging finance regularly.
10. The companies are suggested to use widely the borrowed funds and should try to reduce the fixed charges burden gradually by decreasing borrowed funds and by enhancing the owner's fund. For this purpose, companies may expand their equity share capital by issuing new equity shares.
11. The support and coordination of the government is strongly called for. Infrastructure facilities are needed to be improved for regular supply of raw materials and the final product.
12. The government is suggested to minimize the subsidy and encourage the capital market for the Hometech companies.

CONCLUSION

The purpose of this research project was to highlight the international competitiveness of Indian Hometech industry, which is one of the prominent segments of the Technical

Textiles Industry. The industry holds great significance for its economy. This has been achieved by assessing the literature that exist on this subject and relating that theory to the practical world. With termination of Multi Fibre Arrangement (MFA) on January 1, 2005 a plethora of opportunities came in front of the industry.

The competitiveness of this industry can be studied in both the ways, positively as well as negatively, considering various factors along with it. The industry has immense potential for development and expansion in the near future. The researcher, in this study, has examined the international competitiveness of Indian Hometech industry in textile sector. She has evaluated the competitiveness of India with other countries in terms of its production and performance. There have been several factors (strengths and weaknesses) influencing the performance of Indian Hometech firms. Various inherent strengths include availability of cheap unskilled labour, strong raw material base, growing domestic as well as international market, effective supply chain management and variety of distinct local structure. Whereas the weaknesses which has affected the productivity and have constrained the growth of this industry includes, highly fragmented infrastructure, rigid labour laws, low foreign investment, poor domestic policies and usage of obsolete technology. But with government taking several initiatives to overcome the bottlenecks that hinders the industry's growth, not only the infrastructure should be improved but with increasing education scenario the productivity will also be increased as more skilled labour will be available.

Considering the global scenario, for Indian Hometech industry its major marketplaces are US and Europe. But, India to be the market leader needs to surpass China, which is its biggest competitor. It also needs to provide an edge to cater niche market. To cater this type of market, there is a requirement of continuous innovation process and product differentiation. Since the Indian industry is dominated by small scale firms, it can optimally cater small orders, whereas, China is predominantly concentrating only on the mass production. Another added advantage that India has, is quota restrictions on China that has been applied by US and other countries in the European market.

Earlier, the industry's growth was quite submissive in overall participation in the world textile market. It is still in nascent stage. But today, this industry has a very contemporary outlook, with many effective strategic policies to compete the global market.

The future prospects of the Indian domestic market are also very promising, with strong increase in GDP, rapid expansion of middle income group accompanied with increasing purchasing power of consumers. There are many Indian companies planting their subsidiary units outside the country i.e. US, EU, and UAE. Many mergers and acquisitions are taking place to draw the attention of foreign investors for better infrastructure and technology. By summing it all, India is now completely geared up and is propelling towards humongous growth of the overall industry.

There are various opportunities knocking the doors of this industry with which it can be the market leader worldwide. Therefore, to effectively tackle the weaknesses of this sector the country needs to put high investment in R&D to launch new products and by reducing transaction cost per unit. It also needs to improve their international standards. Another focus area is organising the human resource. For higher productivity it is imperative that the workforce should be skilled and educated. India should also reduce its dependency on the US market, as it will help it to diversify the possibility of risk. Above mentioned all the factors will help the Indian Hometech industry to become a highly competitive player in global market.

Bibliography

Books

1. Bonn, C.V. (2011). Technical Textiles 2011. Deutscher Fachverlag GmbH Technische Textilien/Technical Textiles. Mainzer Landstraße 251 60326 Frankfurt am Main.
2. Bonn, C.V. (2012). Technical Textiles 2012/13. Deutscher Fachverlag GmbH. Technische Textilien/Technical Textiles. Mainzer Landstraße 251 60326 Frankfurt am Main.
3. Horrock, AR and Anand, SC. (2000). Handbook of Technical Textiles. UK: Wood Head Publishing Ltd. & CRC Press LCC.
4. Kothari, C.R. (2004). Research Methodology Methods and Techniques. Second Revised Edition. New Age International (P) Limited Publishers. New Delhi.
5. Koul, L. (2012). Methodology of Educational Research. Vikas Publishing House Private Limited. A-22, Sector-4, Noida - 201 301 (UP), India.
6. Chi, Ting (2010), "An Emperical Study of Trade Competitiveness in the U.S. Technical Textile Industry", Journal of Textile and Apparel Technology and Management, Vol. 6, Issue 4, pp. 1-19.

7. Chugan, Pawan Kumar (2011), "Diversification into Technical Textiles: A Forward Momentum for Indian Textile Industry", *Nirma University Journal of Business and Management Studies,* Vol. 6, Nos. 1 & 2, July-December, pp. 19-33.
8. Porter, M. (1979). How Competitive Forces Shape Strategy. Harvard Business Review, Vol. 57, Issue. 2, pp. 137-145.
9. Besanko, D., Dandrove, D., Shanley M. & Schaefer S. (2003). The Economics of Strategy. John Wiley and Sons, New York.
10. Indian Textile Industry: Porter Analysis. (2006). In equitymaster.com. (The investor's best friend).
11. Texsummit (2007), Home Fashion India, Vol. 6, Issue. 3, pp. 19.
12. Porter (1990) 'The competitive advantage of Nations', London: Mcmillan, pp. 3-100.
13. The Financial Express. (2007). Logistics Firms Suffer due to Poor Port Facilities.
14. Porter's Five Forces for Competitor Analysis & Advantage. (2012, September).

Reports, Surveys and Government Publications

1. Arora Fibres Ltd. (2006). 13th Annual Report 2005-06. Retrieved June 18, 2012.
2. Arora Fibres Ltd. (2007). 14th Annual report 2006-07. Retrieved July 4, 2012.
3. David Rigby Associates. (2010). Technical Textiles and Nonwovens: World Market Forecasts to 2010. Retrieved February 4, 2012.
4. Ginni filaments ltd. (2004). Annual Report 2003-04. Retrieved April 4, 2012.
5. ICRA Management Consulting Services. (2010). Technical Textiles in India – Current and Future Market Scenario. Retrieved September 29, 2012.
6. ICRA Management Consulting Services Limited. (2009). Impact of Economic slowdown on Indian Textile and Clothing Industry. A Study assigned by CITI, Texprocil, AEPC and SRTEPC.

7. Ministry of Textiles. (2011). Annual Report, 2010-11. New Delhi: Ministry of Textiles, Government of India.
8. Ministry of Textiles. (2012). Annual Report, 2011-12. New Delhi: Ministry of Textiles, Government of India.
9. Ministry of Textiles. (2006). Report of the Working Group on Textiles & Jute Industry for the Eleventh Five Year Plan (2007-12). New Delhi: Ministry of Textiles, Government of India.
10. Ministry of Textiles. (2011). Report of the Working Group on Textiles & Jute Industry for Twelfth Five Year Plan (2012-17). New Delhi: Ministry of Textiles, Government of India.
11. Ministry of Textiles. (2010, June 7). National Fibre Policy 2010-11. New Delhi: Ministry of Textiles, Government of India.
12. Ministry of Textiles. (2004, July). Report of the Expert Committee on Technical Textiles: Volume-I. New Delhi: Ministry of Textiles, Government of India, Udyog Bhavan - 110 011.
13. Ministry of Textile. (1999, 3 Aug). Report of the Expert Committee on Textile Policy. New Delhi: Ministry of Textiles, Government of India.
14. Ministry of Textiles. (2007, Aug. 31). National Technology Mission on Technical Textiles. New Delhi: Ministry of Textiles, Government of India.
15. Ministry of Textiles. (2011). Technology Mission on Technical Textiles, Compendium on Centres of Excellence. New Delhi: Ministry of Textiles, Government of India.
16. National Council of Applied Economic Research. (2009, July). Assessing the Prospects for India's Textile and Clothing Sector. Retrieved July 6, 2011.
17. National composites network (NCN). (n.d.). Technical Textiles and Composite Manufacturing. Best Practice Guide. Retrieved July 3, 2011.
18. Office of the Textile Commissioner. (2006). Official Indian Statistics 2005-06. Mumbai: Ministry of Textiles, Government of India.

19. Office of the Textile commissioner. (2009, March). Baseline survey of the Technical Textile Industry in India - Final Report. ICRA Management Consulting Services (IMaCS). New Delhi: Ministry of Textiles, Government of India.
20. Premier Polyfilms Ltd. (2005). Annual Report 2004-05. Retrieved August 10, 2012.
21. Premier Polyfilms Ltd. (2011). Annual Report 2010-11. Retrieved September 4, 2012.
22. Premier Polyfilms Ltd. (2012). Annual Report 2011-12. Retrieved November 6, 2012.
23. Reliance Industries Ltd. (2003). Annual Report 2002-03. Retrieved May 20, 2012.
24. Reliance Industries Ltd. (2007). Annual Report 2006-07. Retrieved June 4, 2012.
25. Reliance Industries Ltd. (2012). Annual report 2011-12. Retrieved December 2, 2012.
26. Technotex. (2011). Compendium on Standards in Technical Textiles Sector.
27. Uniproducts India ltd. (2003). 20th Annual report 2002-03. Retrieved July 4, 2012.
28. Uniproducts India ltd. (2004). 21st Annual report 2003-04. Retrieved July 24, 2012.
29. Reports on Baseline Survey of the Technical Textile Industry in India.
30. Reports of Expert Committee on Technical Textiles.
31. Technical Textiles in India – Current a Future Market Scenario.
32. Final Report on Baseline Survey of the Technical Textile Industry in India (2009), March, Office of the Textile Commissioner.
33. Reports of Expert Committee on Technical Textiles.
34. Specialty Fibre - Section VII, Ministry of Textiles, Government of India, p. 530.
35. Technical Textiles in India – Current a Future Market Scenario, pp. 11-12.

36. http://technotex.gov.in/hometech.html
37. Report of the Expert Committee on Technical Textiles (2004), Vol. 1, Ministry of Textiles, Government of India, New Delhi. p.111.
38. Reports of Expert Committee on Technical Textiles.
39. Specialty Fibre - Section VII, Ministry of Textiles, Government of India, p. 530.
40. Technical Textiles in India – Current a Future Market Scenario, pp. 11-12.
41 http://technotex.gov.in/hometech.html
42. Report of the Expert Committee on Technical Textiles (2004), Vol. 1, Ministry of Textiles, Government of India, New Delhi. p. 111.

Papers

1. Alexander, M. (2010, march 6). Home Textiles- Recent Developments. Retrieved December 11.
2. Anand, S. (2008). Designer Natural Fibre Geotextiles- A New Concept. Industrial Journal of Fibre & Textile Research. Vol. 34. pp. 339-344.
3. Chi, T., Kilduff, P., and Dyer, C. (2005). An Assessment of US Comparative Advantage in Technical Textiles from a Trade Perspective. Journal of Industrial Textiles. Vol. 35. No. 1. 17-37.
4. Chaudhary, A. (2007). Technical Textiles – an Evolving Stage in India. PR Communication Age, Vol. IX. No. 12.
5. Chaudhary, A. and Shahid, N. (2013, March 16). Upcoming Opportunities for the Hometech Textiles Industry in India. Fibre2fashion (Online journal). Saturday, March 16, 2013.
6. Chakrabarty, S. (2008). Indian Technical Textiles Prospects. Asian Technical Textile. January – March. pp. 36-40.
7. Chi, T. (2009). Measurement of Business Environment Characteristics in the US Technical Textile Industry: An Empirical Industry. Journal of Industrial Textiles. Vol. 39. No. 1.

8. Chi, T. (2010). An Empirical Study of Trade Competitiveness in the US Technical Textile Industry. Journal of Textile & Apparel, Technology and Management. Vol. 6. Issue 4.
9. Chaudhary, A. and Shahid, N. (2011, Jan-March). Technical Textile Industry in India: Special Reference to Hometech Industry. International Journal of Business Swot (IJOBS). Vol. IV. No. 1.
10. Chaudhary, A. and Shahid, N. (2012). Growing Importance of Hometech Textiles in India. International Journal of Marketing. Financial Services & Management Research. Volume-1. Issue No. 6.
11. Chugan, P.K. (2011, July - December). Diversification into Technical Textiles: A Forward Momentum for Indian Textile Industry. Nirma University Journal of Business and Management Studies, Vol. 6. No. 1 & 2. pp. 19-34.
12. Chaudhary, A. and Shahid, N. (2012, Nov.). Technical Textiles in India: The Trade Perspective. JM International Journal of Management Research. Volume–2. Issue-6.
13. Dattilo, P.P., King, M.W., Cassill, N.L. and Leung, J.C. (2002). Medical Textiles: Application of an Absorbable Barbed bi-directional Surgical Suture. Journal of Textile & Apparel, Technology and Management. Vol. 2. Issue 2.
14. Dhir, A. (2010). Stimulating Growth for Technical Textiles in India. Retrieved Aug 20, 2010.
15. Gherzi. (2011). Technical Textiles- Raw materials & Technologies. Presented in 5th Asian Textile Conference, Mumbai – March 17-18.
16. Gupta, J.K. (2012). Standardization of Technical Textiles - An Overview. Retrieved May 5, 2012.
17. Hall, M.E. (2010, April). Coating of Technical Textiles. New Cloth Market. Retrieved July 12, 2010.
18. Harrison, P. W. (1979). Cotton in a Competitive World. Textile Institute. Manchester, England. PUB ID: 102-114-679.
19. Heeren, H.V. (2009, June). Nano Technology and Life Style. New Cloth Market.

20. Ibrahim, N.A., Eid, B,M., Hashem, M.M., Refai, R., and El-Hossamy, M. (2010). Smart Options for Functional Finishing of Linen-containing Fabrics. Journal of Industrial Textiles. Vol. 39. No. 3. pp. 233-265.

21. ICRA Management Consulting Services Limited. (2010). Prospects and Opportunities in Technical Textiles: Rajasthan perspective. Presented in Seminar on Emerging Opportunities in Technical Textiles RIICO & FICCI. Retrieved October 15, 2012.

22. Johnson, D.J. (2003). High-tech Fibres for Technical Textiles. Journal of Industrial Textiles, Vol. 32. No. 4.

23. Katiyar, V.S. (2008, Dec.) Home Textile Exports: Design, Issues, Challenges and Opportunities. Retrieved February 25, 2010.

24. Kumar, A. (2008). Technical Textiles. Presented in Technofest'05 SSM College Komarapalayam. Retrieved August 16, 2011.

25. Kothari, V.K. (2009). Technical Textiles - Growth potential and prospects in India. Retrieved May 7, 2010.

26. Marimuthu, M. (2008). Business Opportunity for Nonwovens & Technical Textiles in India. Retrieved March 6, 2010.

27. Mangat, M.M. (2009). Technical Textile: A Promising Future. Retrieved March 7, 2011.

28. Marimuthu, M. (2010). Why should Technical Textiles Grow in India. Fibre 2 fashion (Online Journal). Friday, February 19, 2010.

29. Marmarali, A. (2010). Technical Textile – The Research and Innovation Challenge in the Mediterranean Countries – The Case Study of Turkey. Retrieved October 15, 2012.

30. Ministry of Textiles. (2006, Dec. 12). Use of Geo Textiles. Presentation in the National Advisory Council (NAC) on Technical Textiles with focus on the use of 'Geo Textiles'.

31. Memon, N.A. and Zaman, N. (2007). Pakistan Lags Behind in Technical Textiles. Journal of Management and Social Sciences. Vol. 3. No. 2. pp. 120-127.
32. Nataraj, G. Wadsworth, L.C. and Duckett, K.E. (1994). Non Woven Laminates Containing Cotton for Medical Applications. Journal of Industrial Textiles. Vol. 24. No. 1. pp. 60-76.
33. Nemoz, G. (2001). Applications and Markets of Technical Textiles: Actual Situation and Trends. Retrieved April 11, 2010.
34. Nath, K. (2010, Feb.). Ballistic protection fabric and bullet proof vests. Textile Review. Volume-5. Issue-02.
35. Pal, S. (2010, Aug.). Application of Technical Textiles (part- 1): Agro Textile and Home Textile. Retrieved February 19, 2011.
36. Patel, M. (2010). Technical Textile in India- A Dormant Volcano Prepares to Erupt. Retrieved August 10, 2010.
37. Parthasarthi, V. (2009). Application of Acrylic on Home Textile. Textile Review. Volume-4. Issue-09.
38. Rakshit, A., Hira, M., and Gangopadhyay, U.K. (2007). Technical Textiles: What India Needs to do Now. Textile Review.Vol. 2. Issue 10.
39. Ramkumar, S. (2009, May). Why Technical Textiles is the Next Phase of the Indian Textile Industry. Textile Review. Volume-4. Issue-05.
40. Ramkumar, S. (2009, June). Compelling case for the Technical Textile Sector in India. Textile Review. Volume-4. Issue-06.
41. Ramkumar, S. (2009, Feb). Technical Textiles Cluster Development is the Way for Growth. Textile Review. Volume-4. Issue-02.
42. Ramkumar, S. (2009, Dec). Technical Textiles: Growth Tools for Textile Industry. The Indian Textile Journal. Retrieved January 12, 2011.
43. Ramkumar, S. (2010, Feb). Technical Textiles: Emerging Opportunity. Textile Review. pp. 38-39.

44. Ramkumar, S. (2010, May). Nonwovens and Technical Textiles in India: Current Scenario. USA: Nonwoven & Advanced Materials Laboratory. pp. 101-103.

45. Ramkumar, S. (2010). Technical Textiles in the Changing Economic Landscape. Textile Review Magazine. Vol. 5. Issue-11.

46. Reliance Industries Limited. (2010). Technical Textiles – Growth Potential and Prospects in India. Retrieved September 8, 2010.

47. Ramkumar, S. (2011, Jan). Technical Textiles: A Growing Necessity for the Indian Textile industry. Textile Review. Volume-6. Issue-1.

48. Rakshit, A. (2011). Innovative Polyester Fibres for Future Growth in Technical Textiles. Presented in World Textile Conference on Vision: Textiles 2020: Emerging New Opportunities Worldwide and Challenging Business Strategies held on May 06th & 07th 2011 at Mumbai; organized by The Textile Association, India.

49. Ramkumar, S. (2012, October 30). FDI for Technical Textiles. Textile Review Magazine. Retrieved April 12, 2013.

50. Singh, S. (2008). Emerging Indian Market Trends in Technical Textiles and nonwovens. Retrieved October 16, 2012.

51. Saxena, A., and Srivastava. A. (2010, Feb.). Sunscreen shelter fabric- A Review. Textile Review.Volume-5. Issue-02.

52. Singh, K.V. (2010). India to Grow Faster in Technical Textiles. Textile Review. Retrieved March 7, 2011.

53. Saha, C. (2012, November). Technology Innovation in Home Textile Industry – The Way of Resurgence. New Cloth Market magazine. Retrieved April 19, 2013.

54. Sharan, M. (2013, March 29). Expanding Horizons of Textiles – A Versatile Product. Fibre2fashion. Retrieved April 21, 2013.

55. Shanmugasundaram, O.L. (2009, May). Technical Textiles and Their Applications. The India Textile Journal.

56. Teli, M.D. and Kumar, G.V.N.S. (2007, May-June). Technical Textile-Functional textiles and apparels. Journal of the Textile Association.

57. Uglene, W. (2010, Feb). Recent Advances in Protective Clothing Technology. New Cloth Market. Fibre2fashion. Retrieved April 21, 2013.

58. Vengsarker, S.R. (2009, Dec.). Polypropylene staple fibre for specialized Technical textiles application. Textile Review. Volume-4. Issue-12.

59. Ye, X., Hu, H., and Feng, S. (2008). Development of the Warp Knitted Spacer Fabrics for Cushion Applications. Journal of Industrial Textiles. Vol. 37. No. 3. pp. 213-223.

Web Pages

1. AGA Institute. (n.d.). Calculating Mean and Standard Deviation. In AGA Centre for Quality in Practice. Retrieved October 19, 2011.

2. Ahmadabad Textile Industry's Research Association. (n.d.). Retrieved August 2, 2011.

3. Arora Fibres Limited. (n.d.). In Alibaba.com. Retrieved June 18, 2012.

4. Arora Fibres Limited. (n.d.). In indiainfoline.com. Retrieved June 20, 2012.

5. Arora fibres limited. (n.d.). In reportjunction.com. Retrieved July 2, 2012.

6. Business and Industry. (n.d.). Define Sampling Design. Retrieved October 21, 2011.

7. Business Standard. (2010, July 29, Thursday). Neo Corp Acquires UK Firm.

8. Bathroom Furnishings. (n.d.). In Textile Furnishings Market Place. Retrieved January 23, 2012.

9. Bath Towels. (n.d.). In Textile Furnishings Market Place. Retrieved January 24, 2012.

10. Bed Covers. (n.d.). In Textile Furnishings Market Place. Retrieved January 26, 2012.

11. Bed & Bedding Furnishings. (n.d.). In Textile Furnishings Market Place. Retrieved January 26, 2012.

12. Blind and Curtains. (n.d.). In New Style Blinds & Curtains. Retrieved June 15, 2013.

13. Chair Pads, (n.d.). In Textile Furnishings Market Place. Retrieved February 2, 2012.

14. Circular Mosquito Net. (n.d.). In Fujian Yamei Industry & Trade Co. Ltd. Retrieved June 5, 2013.

15. Coir. (n.d.). In Wikipedia, the Free Encyclopedia. Retrieved April 22, 2012.

16. Commercial Carpet and Rug Construction. (n.d.). In CRI, Carpet and Rug Institute. Retrieved June 22, 2013.

17. Commercial Carpet and Rug Construction. (n.d.). In CRI, Carpet and Rug Institute. Retrieved June 8, 2013.

18. Chaudhary, A. (2007). Technical Textiles – an evolving stage in India. PR Communication age. Volume IX No. 12.

19. Confederation of Indian Textile Industry. (n.d.). Retrieved October 19, 2011.

20. Drawing & Dining Room Furnishings. (n.d.). In Textile Furnishings Market Place. Retrieved April 8, 2012.

21. Dry Filteration. (n.d.). In India Mart. Retrieved August 30, 2013.

22. Economic Times. (2005, Dec. 26). India: Technical Textiles Booming in the Market.

23. Fibre2fashion. (n.d.). About Hometech. Retrieved June 12, 2012.

24. FICCI. (n.d.). FICCI, Industry's voice for policy change. Federation of Indian Chambers of Commerce and Industry. Retrieved December 2, 2011.

25. Funded debt to total capitalization ratio. (n.d.). Retrieved August 11, 2012.

26. Ginni Filaments Limited. (n.d.). In indiainfoline.com. Retrieved April 4, 2012.

27. Ginni Filaments Ltd. (n.d.). In info.shine.com. Retrieved May 9, 2012.

28. Hanung Toys and Textiles Ltd. (n.d.). In (EMIS) Emerging Market Information Service. Retrieved July 24, 2012.

29. Hanung Toys and Textiles. (nd). In The Economic Times. Retrieved September 17, 2012.
30. Human factor: The manufacturers with a difference. (2010). Retrieved July 20, 2010.
31. Hand Towels, (n.d.). In Textile Furnishings Market Place. Retrieved March 9, 2012.
32. Home Textiles (n.d.). In Indian Technical Textile Association. Retrieved September 2, 2013.
33. How to Choose the Right Upholstery Fabric. (n.d.). In DSC Custom Furniture and Design Upholstery. Retrieved June 4, 2013.
34. How to Simplify & Declutter the Toys. (2012). In Small Notebook. Retrieved August 9, 2013.
35. Hometech Auto Fold Curtain. (n.d.). In Hub Pages. Retrieved July 6, 2012.
36. Industrial Research Institute. (2010). Research Management. Michigan: Industrial Research Institute. Retrieved November 25, 2011.
37. Indian Wool Industry. (n.d.). In business.mapsofindia. Retrieved September 14, 2011.
38. India: BCH. (2006. Nov. 6). At IIT Delhi for International Conference on Technical Textiles. Retrieved July 25, 2010.
39. Indian Jute Industries Research Association. (n.d.). About IJIRA. Retrieved March 6, 2011.
40. Indian Technical Textile Association. (n.d.). In ITTA, Voice of Indian Technical Textile Industry. Retrieved May 15, 2011.
41. Inline Active Air Purification HVAC Probes. (n.d.). In breathe-easier.com. Retrieved May 21, 2013.
42. Jaipur Rugs Company Private Limited. (n.d.). In India Mart. Retrieved March 25, 2011.
43. Joshi, R.M. (2005). International Marketing. Oxford University Press. New Delhi and New York. ISBN 0-19-567123-6. Retrieved October 17, 2012.
44. Joshi, R.M. (2009). International Business, Oxford University Press, New Delhi and New York. ISBN 0-19-568909-7. Retrieved September 5, 2012.

45. Joshi A.B. (2011). India's Approach to Technical Textiles. Textile Commissioner. Retrieved January, 2 2012.
46. Karur. (n.d.). In Wikipedia, the Free Encyclopedia. Retrieved February 20, 2011.
47. Kitchen Furnishings. (n.d.). In Textile Furnishings Market Place. Retrieved December 22, 2011.
48. Kusumgar Corporates. (n.d.). Retrieved August 6, 2010.
49. Loyal Textile Mills LTD. (n.d.). Home Textiles. Retrieved June 2, 2011.
50. Mattresses and Pillows. (n.d.). In Borsodchem, Chemistry for Generations. Retrieved August 4, 2013.
51. Modelama Exports ltd. (n.d.). Retrieved January 9, 2011.
52. Man-Made Textiles Research Association. (n.d.). In India Mart. Retrieved September 12, 2011.
53. Market for Technical Textiles seen at $ 20- billion by 2015 (2010, April 21). Technical Textiles. Retrieved September 2, 2010.
54. Mittal, R. (2002, 07 Feb). SASMIRA Makes Major Strides in Technical Textiles. Express Textile.
55. Narendranath, K.G. (1999, June 7, Monday). Research Associations Asked to Submit Reports. Indian Express.
56. Northern India Textile Research Organization. (n.d.). NITRA Profile. Retrieved December 13, 2011.
57. Natural fiber. (n.d.). In Wikipedia, The free encyclopedia. Retrieved January 6, 2011.
58. Obeetee Textiles Pvt. Ltd. (n.d.). Retrieved October 4, 2010.
59. Office of the Textile Commissioner. (n.d.). Agriculture, horticulture and fishing. Office of the Textile Commissioner, Government of India. Retrieved July 12, 2012.
60. Office of the Textile Commissioner. (n.d.). Hometech (Home Textile). Office of the Textile Commissioner, Government of India.
61. Office of the Textile Commissioner. (n.d.). Raw Material Availability. Office of the Textile Commissioner, Government of India. Retrieved March 8, 2012.

62. Office of the Textile Commissioner. (n.d.). The Cotton Textiles Export Promotion Council. Office of the Textile Commissioner, Government of India. Retrieved February 6, 2012.
63. Office of the Textile Commissioner. (n.d.). Federation of Indian Chambers of Commerce and Industry (FICCI). Office of the Textile Commissioner, Government of India. Retrieved October 19, 2012.
64. Office of the Textile Commissioner. (n.d.). Bureau of Indian Standards (BIS). Office of the Textile Commissioner, Government of India. Retrieved January, 20, 2013.
65. Office of the Textile Commissioner. (n.d.). Synthetic & Rayon Textiles Export Promotion Council (SRTEPC). Office of the Textile Commissioner, Government of India. Retrieved February 17, 2013.
66. Office of the Textile Commissioner. (n.d.). Protech (Protective and Safety Clothing and Textiles). Office of the Textile Commissioner, Government of India. Retrieved August 2, 2012.
67. Obeetee. (n.d.). In Freelancers. Retrieved May 2, 2011.
68. Office of the Textile Commissioner. (n.d.). Foreign Investment Framework. Government of India. Retrieved March 23, 2012.
69. Operating Profit. (n.d.). In Investor Words: The Biggest, Best Investing Glossary on the web. Retrieved September 14, 2012.
70. Oracle exports, Home textiles pvt. Ltd. (n.d.). Retrieved December 19, 2010.
71. Polyester. (n.d.). In Wikipedia, the free Encyclopedia. Retrieved November, 5, 2011.
72. Polyester Fiber. (n.d.). In Dream Land Comforts. Retrieved May 3, 2013.
73. Preston, J. (n.d.). Man made fibre. Encyclopædia Britannica. Retrieved December 2, 2012.
74. Production. (n.d.). In Wikipedia, the Free Encyclopedia Online. Retrieved November 28, 2012.

75. Premier polyfilms. (n.d.). In Moneycontrol.com.
76. Premier Polyfilm Limited. (n.d.). In Alibaba.com. Retrieved August 10, 2012.
77. Premier Polyfilm Limited. (n.d.). In Indiainfoline.com. Retrieved July 5, 2012.
78. Percent Increase and Decrease. (n.d.). In Math Goodies. Retrieved July 24, 2011.
79. Queen Bed Tent/ Folded Mosquito Net/ Folding Mosquito Net. (n.d.). Retrieved May 14, 2013.
80. Quilt Covers. (n.d.). In Textile Furnishings Market Place. Retrieved August 25, 2011.
81. Rubberised Coir Mattress, Pillows & Accessories. (n.d.). In Rayaan Enterprises. Retrieved July 13, 2013.
82. Reliance industries. (n.d.). In Moneycontrol.com. Retrieved May 10, 2012.
83. Reliance Industries Limited. (n.d.). In indiainfoline.com. Retrieved May 20, 2012.
84. Reliance Industries Limited. (2012). Reliance Industries Limited. Growth is Life Annual Report: 2011-12). Retrieved June 7, 2012.
85. Reliance Industries Limited. (n.d.). In infoshine.com. Retrieved June 24.
86. Sleepzone. (n.d.). In Bangalore Yellow Pages Online. Retrieved April 4, 2010.
87. Spunlace Non woven Wipes. (n.d.). In DIYTRADE, Global B2B Trading Plateform. Retrieved September 17, 2013.
88. Stuffed Toy. (n.d.). In Wikipedia, The Free Encyclopedia. Retrieved September 13, 2013.
89. Sage Publication. (n.d.). Two Samples Test. Retrieved July, 8, 2012.
90. Synthetic & Art Silk Mills' Research Association. (n.d.). Retrieved November 9, 2012.
91. Shri Lakshmi Cotsyn. (2011). 23rd Annual Report 2010-11, Shri Lakshmi Cotsyn Limited. Retrieved August 6, 2012.

92. Swaminathan, S. (2003, Oct 30). ECTT Priorities Six Major Technical Textiles for Growth. In Express Textile. Para 2. Line 1.

93. Sage Publication. (n.d.). Introduction to Hypothesis Testing (chapter 8). Retrieved August 7, 2013.

94. Standard deviation. (n.d.). In Wikipedia, the free encyclopedia online. Retrieved May, 9, 2012.

95. Student's t-test. (n.d.). In Wikipedia, the free encyclopedia online. Retrieved December 2, 2012.

96. Technotex. (n.d.). List of Manufaturers of Hometech products. Retrieved July 7, 2011.

97. Table Skirting, (n.d.).•In Textile Furnishings Market Place. Retrieved September 15, 2011.

98. Tassels, (n.d.). In Textile Furnishings Market Place. Retrieved January, 10, 2012.

99. The Filling. (n.d.). In decsignco.com. Retrieved May 3, 2013.

100. Technical Textile. (n.d.). In Wikipedia: The Free Encyclopedia. Retrieved March 5, 2010.

101. Technical Textiles sector set to grow phenomenally. (2010, March). In fibre2fashion news desk, India. Retrieved May 2, 2011.

102. TEXPROCIL. (n.d.). TEXPROCIL. The Cotton Textiles Export Promotion Council of India. Govenrment of India. Retrieved January 4, 2013.

103. The Financial Express. (2008, Sept. 25). Sasmira to set up Centre of Excellence for Technical Textiles.

104. The South India Textile Research Association. (n.d.). About SITRA. Retrieved March 18, 2012.

105. Uniproducts India Limited. (n.d.). In indiainfoline.com. Retrieved July 4, 2012.

106. Uniproducts India Ltd. (n.d.). In Wikimapia online. Retrieved June 18, 2012.

107. Uniproducts India. (n.d.). In moneycontrol.com. Retrieved July 13, 2012.

108. Vacuum Cleaner Demo Paper. (n.d.). In Patriot Filter Store. Retrieved September 5, 2013.

109. What is Nylon. (n.d.). In Wise GEEK- clear Answers for Common Questions. Retrieved Aril, 13, 2012.

110. Window Blinds. (n.d.). In Emma's Decoration Blog. Retrieved July 1, 2013.

111. Wool Research Association. (n.d.). Wool Research Association, Setting up of Centre of Excellence in Sportech at Wool Research Association, Thane. Retrieved April 2, 2013.

Business Dailies

1. Business India, New Delhi.
2. Business Standard, Kolkata.
3. Business Today, New Delhi.
4. India Today, New Delhi.
5. Outlook, New Delhi.
6. The Economic Times, New Delhi
7. The Financial Express, New Delhi
8. The Hindu, New Delhi
9. The Hindustan Times, New Delhi
10. The Times of India, New Delhi

Websites

1. http://www.technicaltextile.gov.in/
2. http://technotex.gov.in/
3. http://www.ittaindia.org/
4. http://www.textilesintelligence.com/
5. http://www.fibre2fashion.com/
6. http://articles.economictimes.indiatimes.com
7. http://www.innovationintextiles.com/
8. http://www.intnews.com/TTIBuyersGuide/
9. http://www.leeds.ac.uk/textiles/CTT/
10. http://en.wikipedia.org/wiki/Technical_textile
11. http://www.sgiventure.com/technical_textiles.html
12. http://texmin.nic.in/
13. http://ic.gujarat.gov.in

14. http://www.moneycontrol.com/
15. http://economictimes.indiatimes.com
16. http://www.indianotes.com
17. http://www.researchandmarkets.com
18. http://money.livemint.com
19. http://www.indiainfoline.com
20. http://money.rediff.com
21. http://www.reportjunction.com/

Index

A

Abrasion resistant fabrics, 8

Adhesives fabrics ensure, 9

ANOVA, 61, 63, 64, 65, 66, 67

Anti-allergic andante bacterial textiles, 9

Anti-ballistic textiles, 10

Anti-magnetic textiles and anti radiation fabrics, 9

Anti-static textile prevents, 9

ASTM, 85

ATIRA, 87

Auxetic textiles, 9

B

Bargaining power, 72, 74

Barrier to

competitors, 79

new entrants, 76

substitutes, 78

Bio-textiles, 10

BS, 85

BTRA, 87

BTRA, 87

C

CAGR, 14, 30

CBC, 27, 28, 29, 75

China, 14

Civil engineering, 7

Cleansing textiles, 10

COEs, 87

Competitive analysis of Indian hometech industry, 56-70

hypotheses of the study, 58-60

hypotheses testing, 69

introduction, 56

Porter five competitive forces, 57

study, 57-58

testing of hypothesis, 60-69

Cotton Tape, 40

CRISIL Research estimate, 43

D

Deodorizing or Odor absorbing textiles, 10

DEPB, 22

DIN, 85

DKTE, 87

E

Electronic textiles, 8

EN, 85

Environmental Engineering, 7

EU, 97, 100

F

FIBCs, 17

Fire resistant textile, 8

Five Competitive Forces, 57

Flammability Test Procedure, 84
Flock fabric industry, 42
FTZ, 93

G

GDP, 100
GDP, 2
GHOST, 85
Glister Jute, 77
Growth of the hometech industry in India, 45-55
  hometech textiles, 45-47
  International Tradeoff Indian Hometech Industry, 47-49
  trade of Indian hometech industry with
    China, 52-55
    rest of the world, 49-52
    USA , 52-55
GSM, 36
GST, 22

H

HAVAC filters, 43
HEPA filters, 79
HEPA, 34
Hometech industry in India, 24-44
  blinds, 31-32
  carpet backing cloth, 27-29
  fiberfil, 26-27
  filter fabrics for vacuum cleaners, 35-36
  furniture fabrics, 41-43
  hometech industry, 24-25
  HVAC filters, 32-35
  mattresses and pillows, 36-38
  mosquito nets, 39-40
  nonwoven wipes, 38-39
  overview of hometech products, 26
  products/classification of hometech, 25-26
  stuffed toys, 29-30
HVAC, 34, 35, 51
  filters, 75

I

IITS/Textiles Institutes, 87
India, 45
Indian domestic market, 100
Indian Furniture Market, 41
Indian Hometech Industry, 49, 71, 100
Indian Hometech Product, 53
Indian technical textiles industry, 1-23
  agrotech, 5
  buildtech, 5-6
  clohtech, 6
  factors responsible for slow growth rate of technical textile industry in India, 19-22
  future projections, 17-19
  geotech, 6-7
  hometech, 6
  indutech, 7
  innovations in fibers, textiles and apparels, 8-11
  introduction, 1
  meditech, 5
  mobiltech, 5
  oekotech, 7
  packtech, 5

- protech, 6
- segments in technical textiles, 4-5
- smart fabrics and interactive textiles, 7
- sportech, 5
- technical textiles, 2-4, 11-17
- textiles industry, 1-2
- types of technical textiles, 4

Indian Textile Industry, 1

Insulating textiles, 9

International Consultants, 46

Interpretation, problems and recommendations, 71-100

- interpretation of the hypothesis testing and conclusions drawn, 71-81
- introduction, 71
- major problems, 81-92
  - absence of centres of excellence for home tech textiles, 87
  - absence of research and development, 90
  - bottlenecks for entrepreneurs, 86-87
  - cheaper imported goods, 91
  - depreciation of US dollar, 89
  - entry of new units, 90
  - fluctuations in cotton/ cotton yarn prices, 88-89
  - foreign exchange fluctuations and interest rate risk, 92
  - global recession, 89
  - higher cost of raw material, 82-83
  - increase in fuel prices, 89
  - lack of
    - awareness, 81-82
    - demand, 82
    - processes, machineries and equipment, 84-85
    - quality assurance, 86
    - regulatory norms by the government, 84
    - research and development, 83
    - skilled labour or manpower, 83-84
    - technology and know-how, 85
    - testing facilities, 85-86
  - low value imports from other Asian and south east Asian countries, 90-91
  - multi fiber agreement, 81
  - quota regime for exports of textile/clothing, 88
  - tsunami in Japan-2011, 91
  - unhealthy competition from unorganized sector, 89-90
- recommendations and suggestions, 92-97
- reducing
  - bargaining power of
    - buyers, 94
    - suppliers, 92-93

competitive rivalry between existing players, 96-97
threat of substitutes, 96
treat of new entrants, 94-95
suggestions for improving the economic position of hometech industry in general, 97-98

IT/ITEs, 9, 25

K

Karnataka, 22

L

Ludlow Jute, 77
Luminescent and reflective textiles, 9-10

M

Marine Engineering, 7
MFA, 88
Multi Fibre Arrangement (MFA), 99
Multifunctional textiles, 9

N

Nano fibers, 8
National Building Code, 22
NELCO, 42
NITRA, 87
Noise Vibration and Harness, 5
Nylon Mosquito Net, 40

P

Porter Five Forces Model, 71
Porter Five Forces, 57
Porter, Micheal, 56
Product Category, 61, 62, 65
PSF, 26
PVC, 42

R

Recommendations, 71-100
Reliance Industries Limited, 27

S

SASMIRA, 87
SEZ, 93
SFIT, 7
Shape memory polymer, 10
SITRA, 87
SKAPs, 17
Smart or intelligent textiles, 8
Soluble textiles, 10
Stuff toys, 74

T

TE Textiles Exchange, 23
Technical Textile Industry in India, 80
Texas Tech University, 11
Textile Commissioner, 46
TT, 14
TUFS, 15, 85

U

UAE, 100
Ultra-fine textiles, 8
US, 100

V

Valentine Day, 29
VAT, 22

W

Waterproof textiles, 10, 11

❑ ❑ ❑ ❑ ❑ ❑